THE ORGAN AS MUSICAL MEDIUM

Zwolle, Michaelskerk. Arp and Frans Caspar Schnitger, 1718-21; restored, D. A. Flentrop, 1953-55.

THE

ORGAN

AS

MUSICAL

MEDIUM

JOHN FESPERMAN

COLEMAN - ROSS COMPANY, INC.

NEW YORK

TO GUSTAV LEONHARDT

ACKNOWLEDGMENTS

The author's debt of gratitude is deep and owed to many: to Mr. Gustav M. Leonhardt for his help in locating out-of-the-way information, especially with reference to restored and altered instruments; to Messrs. Rudolph von Beckerath, E. Power Biggs, Charles Fisk, D. A. Flentrop, Arthur Howes, Noel Mander, Robert Noehren, Melville Smith, and Donald Willing for photographs; and to Miss Gale McGovern of the publisher's music research staff for her guidance in the final stages of revision and editing of the manuscript.

Finally, special thanks are due to Miss Wobbina J. M. Kwast of the Nederland-Amerika Instituut in Amsterdam, and Mr. Jaap van der Waarde of Zwolle, custodian of the Michaelskerk and its monumental organ.

J. F.

FOREWORD

IT IS gratifying to witness the tremendous growth of interest in the organ since World War II, not only as an instrument of the church but also as an artistic musical medium. The paths to historical organs throughout Europe have become crowded with curious young musicians eager to seek an instrument which will justify the musical demands of its great literature. We have seen how the "modern organ" as it emerged in the early years of the 20th century dangerously forsook its heritage. It all but lost its shape and sound, and its muddy tones turned away many gifted students who hastened to seek out a more sympathetic musical medium to fulfill their urge for expression. Happily, this era is fast passing on, and the organ is regaining its former artistic stature.

Organists and students everywhere will be grateful for this volume, which is one of the first in modern times to set forth a true description of the organ and the traditional principles which underlie its design and construction. The obvious enthusiasm of the author, together with the photographs of great organs, should prove an inspiration to the reader.

ROBERT NOEHREN

CONTENTS

LIST OF PLATES

PART ONE

1 ORIENTATION

THIS BOOK is an attempt to develop an understanding of the organ as an appropriate and distinctive means for making music. Much of the material treated here was previously available only in widely scattered places, often untranslated, and sometimes completely inaccessible to practicing musicians. It is hoped that the usefulness of this volume will lie in its assembling in a meaningful way basic information about organ design, supported by dispositions, photographs, and descriptions. These are derived for the most part from the author's personal experience with the instruments discussed, which are intended to represent a compendium of masterpieces.

Although some of the most important music in existence was written for the organ, it has become the most misunderstood and misrepresented of instruments. If it is to return to a secure position of musical respectability, there is a need to re-establish a concept of the organ as a distinctive musical medium.

To do this, it is first necessary to understand the instrument historically, to discover how it was understood by its greatest builders, players, and composers, for the organ is *the* historical instrument. Despite the efforts of a small vanguard of devoted players and builders, the paucity of artistic imagination, musicianship, and craftsmanship currently expended on the organ—especially in the United States—is testimony that something vital is missing: the instrument has somehow lost its identity as a unique musical medium.[1]

---

[1]Walter Holtkamp (he died February 11, 1962) was the first American investigator to apply fresh ideas and imagination to organ building, and to turn his attention to European practices, both early and recent. His Positiv division for the instrument in the Cleveland Museum of Art (1933) marks the beginning of the renaissance of ideas in design in the United States. (See his *Present-Day Trends in Organ Building*, Cleveland, 1940, published by the author.) Mr. Holtkamp's approach is solidly musical; although he

Trying to uncover basic principles is more productive than an effort merely to reproduce an instrument of a particular period or master builder.[2] As will be seen later, the presence of similar but not identical masterpieces from different times and places constitutes a frustrating dilemma for the informed builder, performer, or composer.

For ideal rendering of the legitimate repertoire, a somewhat different instrument would be necessary for nearly every major composer of organ music. When chronologically and geographically defined musical styles are taken into account, this ideal requirement becomes even clearer. Yet regardless of artistic intentions, a practical attempt to fulfill this demand could be seriously contemplated only by a museum.

What are the physical characteristics which give the organ identity as a musical instrument, characteristics which are independent of the stylistic peculiarities of a given builder or the taste of period and place? What qualities make the piano, the violin, or the harpsichord uniquely expressive, each in its own very special and idiomatic way? To understand the organ as a distinctive medium it is helpful to compare it to other musical instruments.

Musical Performance and Instrument Design

There are two trends in the field of keyboard music which have prompted this book. They were observed in the course of active musical performance and study of the keyboard repertoire and keyboard instruments—not only modern ones, but those which

---

has declined in most instances to build mechanical action or cases around his instruments, he has used slider windchests, and has argued cogently for bringing the player and the listener "into a more intimate contact with the instrument." He has also shown great skill in arranging uncased pipework with an eye to both architectural design and its logical relationship to different divisions of the organ. See also his article in *The Contemporary American Organ* by William H. Barnes (New York, J. Fischer & Bro., 1937), pp. 173-176.

[2]Although completely authentic reproduction is perhaps unwise and even impossible, an attempt at careful reproduction may be a necessary first step towards understanding a stylistic or technical aspect of the work of a master builder.

were contemporary with the great repertoire of the 17th and 18th centuries.

Musical Performance. Musicians are too often inclined to be superficial about *style* in the performance of music written before 1800. This is due perhaps to the romantic fallacy that "expression" means only subjective self-expression, and perhaps to the bloodless, pedantic manner in which such music is often played. The performer frequently appraches "old" music with reverence, but without understanding that its expressive qualities do not always fit 19th-century attitudes. He frequently fails roundly because he ignores or cannot conceive of stylistic peculiarities which are as essential to the music as the notes themselves. For instance, there is a tendency to feel that by obeying a few pat rules drawn from an editor's introduction, one has solved such intricate matters as ornamentation in Bach, or Couperin's *notes inégales,* or the rhythmic alterations and arpeggiations in Frescobaldi. The fact is that the performer must become immersed in the music itself, and come to grips with the basic components of the style. That this has to do with true musical expression and enjoyment, and is not mere antiquarianism, can be demonstrated by an informed and sensitive player.

The new face which a composition assumes when played with the requisite freedom and stylistic nuance based on a thorough understanding of the characteristic medium of a composer and his period as well as of the instrument in question, is ample reward for the arduous and subtle task of unraveling the eccentricities of his style.

Instrument Design. The second tendency is to compromise in the *design* of keyboard instruments. Because of its size and complicated structure, this is especially true of the organ. Such compromise arises from a basically nonmusical approach, and from a lack of historical understanding.

The current renaissance in organ building and the recent interest in the whole keyboard repertoire before 1750 have already produced better contemporary instruments and many more satisfactory performances of the music. They have also given rise to confusion about instruments and musical styles, heightened by a host of well-meaning enthusiasts whose opinions are often based more on a fashionable antiquarianism than on documentation, artistic experience, and discrimination. This is a consequence of ignoring the historical side of the musical question—forgetting that most of the instruments of *historical* importance are in Europe. They must be visited, examined, heard and played—not once but many times—before an adequate background for either performance or instrument making can be acquired. The matter is too complicated to be solved by reading books, hearing recordings, or even making a hasty trip abroad to spend a few hours at two or three famous organs (which may or may not be what they were originally). Some very discerning questions in regard to any 17th- or 18th-century organ must be satisfactorily answered before it can be considered representative of the best work of the time. (See Chapter 6.)

Significance of Early American Organs

Things would indeed be easier for American players and builders if there were more early instruments to be seen and played within their own country. The largest and most important organs still existing on this continent are perhaps the least accessible: the 17th- and 18th-century Spanish instruments in Mexico, notably the two in the Cathedral in Mexico City. The earlier of these, built in Spain about 1690,[3] has been investigated and photographed by the American builder Charles Fisk,[4] who has described it as almost entirely unaltered and "amazingly beautiful to both the eye and the ear." It has a double-fronted case (speaking into the choir and the nave), with the *en chamade* reeds typical of Spanish instruments of the period. It contains about sixty stops, a Pedal compass of one "short" octave (but this division includes reeds at 16', 8', and 4' pitch!) and three keyboards, one of which controls two divisions of the organ.

The Cathedral's second organ, slightly later in date, was probably built in Mexico, using the 1690 instrument as a model, al-

---

[3] In 1688, the Cathedral made its request for the organ to the Church authorities in Spain.

[4] The description given here was supplied by Mr. Fisk. The keyboard ranges of the organ were as follows: 27 notes for the top keyboard, CC-d''' for the middle one, and CCC-d''' (with bottom octave only duplicating Pedal) for the bottom one.

though it is not a copy. It was constructed by José Nazarre; the builder of the first organ is not known.

These resplendent instruments far surpassed in size and magnificence anything imported into the English colonies in the early days, and prompted the beginning of what must have been a thriving organ-building trade in 18th-century Mexico. Fortunately, a good number of these instruments still survive.[5]

The first organs in what is now the United States were based for the most part on English ideas. The work of John Snetzler, who was in London from 1747 to 1781, is an example of the best of these. A German by birth, Snetzler settled in England after an apprenticeship with J. C. Müller, and became that country's most notable 18th-century builder. His instruments, in the English fashion, had no pedals; they consisted of a rather complete (by northern European standards) Great, and a Swell (occasionally a Choir) of rudimentary disposition, consisting almost entirely of 8' and 4' registers. Since it is very likely that Handel used instruments built by Snetzler, his work has special significance in relation to proper performance of Handel's music. For the organ concerti, single keyboard "cabinet organs" are probably most typical, and Snetzler made many of these.

Unfortunately, of the relatively few organs made in or imported to North America in the 18th century, almost nothing original remains aside from case work.[6] These cases bear testimony to the elegant taste of the men who built them and the churches which bought them, especially when we consider that a remote

---

[5]Colonial Mexican organ building and the instruments in the Cathedral in Mexico City are discussed in Pál Kelemen, *Baroque and Rococo in Latin America* (New York, Macmillan, 1951), pp. 225-238.

[6]The organs at Christ Church, Boston (the "Old North" Church), made in Boston by Thomas Johnston in 1759; Trinity Church, Newport, Rhode Island (made in London by Richard Bridge in 1733); St. Michael's Church, Charleston, South Carolina (made in London by John Snetzler in 1768); and Christ Church, Philadelphia (made in Philadelphia by Philip Feyring in 1766)—all represent surviving 18th-century examples of largely unaltered cases, which now house modern instruments with virtually none of the original mechanism or pipes. It is not certain in every instance whether the organ builder himself made the case, or whether it was made by someone else with the builder's collaboration. (See Ellinwood, *The History of American Church Music*, Chapter 7.)

province was hardly the most likely field for organ builders. Obviously, the rigid exclusion by the Puritan congregations of "frivolous" objects like organs reduced the number of possible places for instruments; but they were in demand among the Lutherans of Pennsylvania and the Anglicans of the southern and northern coasts.

It was only after the first quarter of the 19th century that organs began to be produced in quantity (if not in quality) in this country by such men as Henry Erben, Thomas Hall, E. and G. G. Hook, Jardine, J. H. and S. Odell, William Johnson, Hilborne Roosevelt, and George Hutchins. The bulk of the ideas of American organ builders was of English inspiration, although a few imported instruments, such as the one made in 1863 by the German firm of Walcker for the Boston Music Hall, undoubtedly had some influence; and the Germanic ideas of David Tanneberger of Saxony found expression in at least twenty-four instruments in Pennsylvania.[7]

However good the mechanical workmanship of these men was (and much of it was excellent[8]), and however favorably some of their instruments compare tonally with 20th-century organs, they were participants in a kind of artistic tragedy. Strongly influenced by the English conception of the organ as an instrument whose main purpose was to accompany the Anglican service, these builders supplied an insatiable market for organs in 19th-century America. The tragedy is that they lived and worked in a musical era when the organ was not a significant concern of the best composers and performers, and when its formal identity—so clearly established in the 17th and 18th centuries—had become seriously obscured. A truly great repertoire simply did not exist, and what

----

[7]Tanneberger worked with Johann Gottlob Klemm in Bethlehem, Pennsylvania, from 1749 to 1762, and then in Lititz until 1804. One of his organs may be seen in York, Pennsylvania (now owned by the York Historical Society). See Ellinwood, *op. cit.*, pp. 54 ff.

[8]Because the slider chests and often the key action (when carefully regulated and balanced) of a great many 19th-century American organs are frequently in good condition or can be repaired inexpensively, it is always wise to investigate the possibility of retaining this mechanism when there is a question of improving such instruments. It is better to replace the pipes and retain the action than to waste money on electrification.

there was had been superseded by interest in the repertoire of other media, notably the piano and the orchestra. Therefore, the design of their organs presents a curious unwieldiness when performance of the best literature is attempted. The conditions which might have stimulated the production of masterpieces of organ building were absent: a tradition of great players, and a significant idiomatic repertoire related to instruments which had distinctive formal and stylistic identity.

ARTISTIC AND PRACTICAL PROBLEMS

TO DEAL coherently with the organ and its repertoire, both artistic and practical problems must be faced—although the latter are relevant only insofar as they further musical ends. The key to adequate understanding lies in seeing these problems within their historical context and studying the solutions which were devised by earlier builders and designers.

Musical Purpose

Ever since the introduction of systems for keyboard notation, the organ has been of considerable importance as a musical medium. Its artistic *raison d'être* has always been to allow the ideas of the musicians who wrote for it or improvised upon it to be realized and heard. At times it has been of central significance: Frescobaldi, Scheidt, Sweelinck, and, later, Buxtehude and Bach considered the organ a worthy vehicle for some of their most exalted ideas. They also excelled as performers, and the organ was often the instrument they preferred. Despite changes in taste and popular esteem, it has never disappeared completely from the musical scene—although it has come close to disappearing when its musical individuality has been ignored or misunderstood.

From the musician's standpoint, the organ is not merely a "functional" instrument. It exists, as far as the artist is concerned, to make music, and not to perform a task which is primarily functional or ceremonial. True, much that has been written for the organ has been occasioned by a demand for music within a specific context, such as the corporate worship of God, or the celebration of some great event, or even communal or private lamentation for a great tragedy. It is also true that to divorce music from its original surroundings invites confusion as to style and manner of performance, and expressive communication. The same confusion can also arise in that 19th-century institution, the formal "concert," especially when it consists of a potpourri of works from different periods and styles. But whether an instrument is functional in any extramusical way is irrelevant if the ultimate aim is a musical, an artistic one.

The organ may be classified as a "church" instrument,[1] or as an instrument for the court, or even as a chamber music instrument, when 18th-century "house" organs are considered.[2] *Musically,* this is of no matter. The central question for the musician is, Will the music stand as a work of art? And, in the case of the organ, the corollary is, Will the instrument realize the music? And to realize the music adequately means to do so in terms of what its creator intended us to hear.

The Practical Problem

Expense. The practical problem is twofold. The first half involves the unfortunate fact that organs are expensive. Being the most complex of musical instruments in size and resources, they require large amounts of space and can be enormously unwieldy. Experimentation means large outlays of money and effort—many times more than would be required for the experimental design and construction of smaller instruments. No matter how good or bad an organ may be artistically, once it is built its owner must tolerate its faults for many years to come.

---

[1] Albert Schweitzer notes that the original liturgical context of Bach's cantatas no longer exists, and he argues convincingly that such music transcends any limitations of time and place. His comments also make sense when applied to the organ repertoire. "Bach, like every lofty religious mind, belongs not to the church but to religious humanity." Schweitzer, *J. S. Bach,* Vol. I, pp. 263 ff.

[2] Good examples of such organs are the one-manual, divided-keyboard instruments without Pedal, especially popular in England and northern Europe in the second half of the 18th century. Several by John Snetzler (London, 1747-1781), including one which possibly belonged to George III and may have been used by Handel, are to be seen in the collection of the London builder Noel Mander. (Disposition No. 16, and Plate VIII.)

This becomes highly relevant when it is realized that, especially in the United States, there is confusion as to whether the organ has "form" in the sense that other instruments have. Until this is resolved—not just in theory but in the actual practice of organ building—there will continue to be a lack of artistic sense of direction on the part of both builder and player. What *is* a musically adequate organ, one which can be termed a genuine musical instrument? It is one which has formal identity as an integrated instrument and which will faithfully render the intentions of the composer who understands it. Nothing else is required of it as an artistic medium.

But if the builder has no clear artistic intentions, the result is usually a practical as well as a musical dilemma: an unwieldy, expensive machine which will not meet the musical requirements served on it. To be practical as well as musical, then, it is necessary first to discover what kind of instrument will fulfill legitimate musical demands.

Learning from Earlier Organs. The second half of the practical problem is to find out historically what kind of instrument was contemporary with the music which will be played upon its modern counterpart. Fortunately this can be done, although it is a far from simple task. Good examples are still extant of instruments by leading organ makers of the past which were intended to meet the artistic demands of the best contemporary composers and players. Careful investigation shows that these composers and these builders had a clear and distinctly musical idea of what form the organ should take. Certainly it is not realistic to expect to find these instruments precisely as their makers left them two or more centuries ago; many have been altered beyond recognition. But repeated study of a group of instruments, playing the appropriate repertoire upon them, enables the researcher to learn how to separate the original from the altered, and to recognize the basic ideas and principles as well as the stylistic marks of different builders.

One Organ for the Entire Repertoire?

At this point, the complicating factor mentioned earlier arises. Music of great artistic merit has been written in many different styles in different periods. All of this music, if it genuinely fits the nature of the organ (if it is "idiomatic"), has some common characteristics. But not all of it makes identical demands on the resources of the instrument; the music of Frescobaldi needs some different sounds from that of Bach. This complication has practical and artistic importance: if one instrument cannot play *all* of the music from various periods and in various styles, must the performer have a different instrument for each period and style?

The only answer which would be completely defensible from a musical standpoint is "Yes." For the simple reason that the organ of Sweelinck or Bach differs from that of Frescobaldi or Couperin, it will not render authentically the music of these composers. Their compositions were intended for instruments not of a different name, but at least of different specific resources.

Even assuming the solution of formidable artistic problems, the financial obstacles involved would allow very few organists to have at their disposal a "Bach" organ as well as a "Sweelinck" organ or a "Frescobaldi" organ—to mention a few examples of different organ-building styles.

A more realistic approach is to inquire whether one of these instruments in a clearly defined style can be selected—one for which much idiomatic music of the highest caliber has been created, one which possesses the essential musical characteristics of an organ. If this can be done, the player must still be aware of its limitations when he uses it for music in different styles. If the instrument is a classic example of a highly refined style of organ building, it can be used to render *musically* (if not "authentically") works which may have been intended for earlier or different organs, provided that the music itself is idiomatic and suits the nature of the instrument. This approach assumes similar underlying principles of design for the several "classic" instruments of various periods; but it also makes a much more dangerous assumption: that the player will not succumb to the temptation (prompted by still prevalent 19th-century tastes and attitudes towards performance practices) to lump together all organ music composed before 1800 as "old" or "baroque" music. Such an attitude only insures that important stylistic differences will be ignored; it also frequently implies that such music, however quaint or charming, is devoid of expression.

The inevitable question of the player or builder who merely wants to satisfy the public is, "Why not have one instrument which, because of a compromise disposition or 'all-purpose' design, will make an attempt at playing the whole repertoire?" In the first place, an artistic judgment needs to be made on segments of the repertoire which may not be worth playing or may be so unidiomatic as to make their validity as organ music questionable. In the second place, experience has demonstrated that artistic needs are more satisfactorily met by an instrument (1) which is coherently designed within the limits of one style and which has distinctive identity as an organ, and (2) which is able to play some important segments of the repertoire authentically, rather than none of the repertoire with true authenticity of style and sound. Because of its clear identity as a unique musical medium, one of these organs will be seen to have an especially valid claim to the position of model, to which others can be instructively compared.

Such an instrument, because it adheres to basic principles of style and design, will play the legitimate repertoire more musically than a so-called all-purpose organ. Either an instrument has formal stylistic integrity, or it is merely a mechanical contrivance. How unsatisfactory is the singer who uses the same style for Brahms lieder and Bach arias! Even though he has but one voice, the artist does not confuse the two styles. The "all-purpose" idea results in an instrument which is no longer musical, which is a little bit of everything but not completely in any one style, and therefore has no identity as a medium—or as a work of art.

A specific example may reinforce this point, which seems so obvious in many other areas of art but often escapes organ builders. A "North German style" main division loses its significance when there is no Positiv or Brust divisions to complement it, or when the Pedal disposition (or scaling or location) is not appropriate. A 19th-century French Swell division, with appropriate reeds and low mixtures, and an 18th-century German Great, with higher mixtures and transparent flue work coupled with an English cathedral-style Pedal, have the unhappy fate of not belonging together. They do not constitute an expressive and integrated instrument, but a conglomeration as eclectic as a harpsichord adapted with piano strings to play Brahms. Such patchwork might at first seem to the obliging builder to make the organ more versatile. Even if it achieved this, it would be a feat of questionable artistic merit; however, it succeeds mainly in precluding truly authentic performance of the music of any period or style. The essence of the artist's task, when working in classic media, is not to innovate but to perfect—thus transcending place and time.

"MUSICAL" AND "INSTRUMENT"

THE DIFFERENCE between a machine and an instrument lies in the factor of intimate control which allows *expressiveness*. The word "machine" suggests such terms as precision, rigidity, mechanical, automatic; one does not readily conceive of an "expressive machine." The word "instrument" suggests precision and flexibility; in the term "musical instrument," the idea of expressiveness is inescapable. A phonograph and a music box are "musical machines": whatever expressive qualities they have are locked in, preset, not variable, except in a mechanical, remote-control kind of way.

Obviously, a musical instrument employs mechanical principles in order to produce sound. But in the hands of a master, the mechanical contrivances are kept as simple as possible once this function is accomplished[1]—for the good reason that they quickly become cumbersome or artificial, and inhibit rather than facilitate expressive control. The violin and the recorder are among the least complicated instruments, consisting of only the tone-producing essentials without "convenient" refinements. Mechanical additions have been omitted consciously or intuitively by the makers, because they would interpose between the player and his instrument. The human voice is obviously the only "immediate" instrument, directly controlled by the singer. The piano and the harpsichord, depending on more involved mechanical equipment to produce a tone, are less immediate.

---

[1]It is significant that during the 18th century few instruments were built which could be called large by modern standards. The organ at Zwolle, the Schnitger family's largest, had 63 stops; it is one of a very few with four keyboards. D. A. Flentrop expresses the idea of control in terms of ships: a steamship is "operated" by its captain by remote control, whereas a small sailboat is intimately controlled, almost played upon by its master.

But with each of these instruments, after a mechanism sufficient to produce the desired tone-color efficiently was perfected, the experimental refinements ended, and the instruments assumed the classic forms which we now associate with a Bechstein piano or a Blanchet harpsichord. From roughly 1500 to 1775, this was also true of the organ—until the advent of "symphonic" and unidiomatic writing, pneumatic action, and later, electric action.

Characterizing the Musical Instrument

It is enlightening to look at the characteristics common to instruments other than the organ, such as the piano, harpsichord, flute, or violin, in an effort to see whether these characteristics apply to the organ of today or of past times.

1. Keyboard, fingerboard, and other means of expressive control are always kept as uncomplicated as possible, with the most direct connection possible between player and sound-producing components.[2] The violin and the flute are perhaps the clearest examples. In these instruments the player controls to as great an extent as is physically possible the manner of initiation and release of tones, their quality, dynamic intensity, duration (and alteration during duration), and pitch. With the piano or harpsichord the player cannot vary the pitch of a given note, although he can produce pitch variations with the clavichord. He loses other regulating powers, also, but he can control dynamic intensity and duration. He can influence the kind of attack and, with the harpsichord in some cases, the kind of release of tones, an idiomatic advantage often exploited by composers.

2. Any "convenience" which would inhibit the expressive control or violate the logic of structure has been discarded by players and instrument makers, or grafted on after the end of a period of refining and perfecting of a recognizable form.[3]

---

[2]The removal of organ keyboards from the case of the instrument is a modern practice with no artistic justification.

[3]An illustration of a structural alteration at the end of a period of refinement is the jalousie attached by Burkat Tschudi [Shudi] (1702-1773) to

3. Expressive ability and structural logic, not size or convenience, have consistently been the chief consideration of both instrument makers and players. Extensive physical expansion has produced confusion as to the basic pinciples of design, and museums could be filled with rejected experimental versions of instruments before their classic dimensions have been achieved. Ultimately the piano, harpsichord, violin, and other instruments have settled down to optimum proportions.

4. Each of these instruments, the harpsichord being most comparable to the organ, has both sound-producing mechanism and resonator included in the same case, which thus becomes an integral part of the instrument.

Characteristics of a Masterpiece: Zwolle

The organ, too, after much experimenting and refining, emerged as an instrument of distinctive form. With what factors—proportional, tonal, and structural, as well as expressive—have great organ builders concerned themselves? A study of selected instruments, especially in northern Europe, but also in England, Spain, France, Austria, and Switzerland, has convinced the writer that certain matters were always dealt with similarly by master builders—and with the utmost care. Our general explanation of these components below takes as an example one of Europe's most monumental instruments, one which epitomizes the organ-build-

---

harpsichords he made in England during the latter part of the 18th century. A well-preserved example is in the Fenton House Museum, London.

Tschudi is credited with the invention of the Venetian swell in 1769; it was soon applied to organs in England by Samuel Green (1740-1796). A sliding shutter was apparently first used by Abraham Jordan in 1712 for an organ in St. Magnus' Church, London. The "swell" effect was known in Spain at least as early as 1703 (Seville Cathedral) and doubtless was occasionally employed by inventive builders elsewhere even earlier.

In 19th-century French organs the enclosed *Récit* division became standard. Often a "hitch-down" pedal controlled the mechanism so that it was used either open or shut, rather than for gradual crescendo effects. (See W. L. Sumner, *The Organ,* pp. 94, 182-184.)

ing style indigenous to the music of Bach, a contemporary of its builders, Arp and Frans Caspar Schnitger.[4]

This is the organ in the Michaelskerk in the Hanseatic city of Zwolle. It exhibits the tonal scheme of the Schnitger tradition carried to its logical conclusion: four keyboards and Pedal, a total of 63 registers. It is the largest instrument made by the Schnitgers.[5]

The distinctive characteristics of the Schnitger instruments, exemplified not only at Zwolle, but also at Alkmaar,[6] Steinkirchen, Noordbroek, Stade, Hamburg, Cappel, Uithuizen, and elsewhere, were these:

1. *Case and Visual Form.* The instruments had *visual form* derived from structural and musical requirements. There was a case for the pipes of each division, related in dimensions and location to the other parts of the organ. Large instruments included a main keyboard division, based on 8' pitch; a Rückpositiv based on 4' pitch; a Brustwerk based on 2' pitch; and a Pedal division based on 16' pitch. High "towers" for the Pedal pipes stood on either side of the main case; the main division and Brustwerk cases were

---

[4]In 1717, Bach inspected the new organ by Johann Scheibe in the Paulinerkirche, Leipzig, and wrote a report to the congregation calling attention to the lightness of action, adequate wind supply, and prompt speech of reed pipes. The disposition of this organ was very similar to that of Schnitger instruments (Disposition No. 13). In 1720, Bach applied eagerly for the position of organist at the Jacobikirche in Hamburg, where there was an organ by Arp Schnitger (1692), but he was bypassed in favor of another applicant. The organ Bach played at the Thomaskirche in Leipzig also presents a very Schnitger-like disposition; it had been rebuilt by Scheibe in 1721, two years before Bach's arrival.

For further discussion of these instruments, and of Bach's connection with them, see Hans David and Arthur Mendel, *The Bach Reader,* p. 76, and Werner David, *Bachs Orgeln,* pp. 52 ff. and 94 ff.

[5]Arp Schnitger (1648-1719), succeeded by his sons Frans Caspar and Johann Georg, who were in turn succeeded by A. A. Hinsch. The latter's work is represented by impressive instruments in the Netherlands such as those at Leens (1733), Midwolda (1772), and Bolsward (1776-1781).

[6]The organ at Alkmaar has a main case from the 17th century by van Campen; some of the pipes also date from this earlier instrument, which originally had no Pedal, put possessed a 26' Prestant on the Hoofdwerk (ending at FF). However, in 1725 the Schnitgers completely revised and rebuilt the instrument, retaining the Rugwerk case (*c.* 1645) as well as the main case, which consequently lacks the Pedal towers usually associated with Schnitger cases.

directly above the keyboards, with Rückpositiv case directly behind the player on the rail of the gallery in which the organ
was almost inevitably placed, while its action ran conveniently
beneath the floor, and its sound projected well into the nave.
Just as the piano has the familiar "wing" form dictated by placement of soundboard, strings, and keyboard, so the organ has its
own logical form, which is the same for organs of any style-period,
not merely of the "baroque."

The physical dimensions of each Schnitger case corresponded
to the basic *pitch* of the division, with the main case in front of the
player, Pedal tower cases to the left and right, other cases directly
above or below the main case, and the Positiv case behind the
player. Ideally, a three-keyboard organ possessed three distinct
cases (plus the two Pedal towers for "C" and "C-sharp" sides),
all of different heights: 16′ for Pedal, 8′ for main division, 4′ for
Positiv, 2′ for Brustwerk. This gave each division its own unique
resonating character, derived partly from the case itself; a wood
which resonates freely, such as spruce, was preferred for the case.
High and remarkably shallow,[7] the total case had only the front
side open, with the top and other sides closed. The reason for this
was practical as well as musical, since it helped to protect the pipework from dust, and at the same time to blend and project the
sound. In the front of the case was displayed the basic "Prestant"[8]
rank of open principal pipes,[9] on which the scales and voicing for
the rest of the division were based.[10] These handsome pipes were
made of pure tin, or as nearly pure as possible, depending on
the cost of the instrument. Each case was open only on the
front side; it normally had side walls, separating it from the

---

[7]Cases were rarely as much as 4′ deep, even in very large organs; the depth
of the Zwolle main case is 3′6″.

[8]This term is explained on page 21.

[9]It is sometimes helpful in dating the case pipes to note whether they pos-
sess rounded *labia* (as at Zwolle), common in the 18th century in northern
Europe, or pointed (spitz) *labia,* typical of much pipework before 1700.
In rebuilt instruments, case front pipes are apt to be older than those inside
the organ.

[10]This may be seen in the photographs of Schnitger instruments (Plates III,
IV and VI).

other divisions, so that each resonated as an individual instrument. Most important, Schnitger's cases stood free from the wall. There were two reasons for this: (1) the case, which is part of the organ, could resonate more freely, just as in other instruments, when not attached to a rigid mass; (2) it assured access for tuning, especially of the reeds which are to be found at the back side of the chest (except in the Brustwerk, where they would be reached more easily at the front, since the action for the main division passed immediately behind the Brustwerk chest).[11]

Although decoration of the outside of the case followed the specifications of the architect and the taste of the times, its interior dimensions were always in accordance with the tonal design and the scales of the organ—not only in the work of Schnitger but of earlier builders as well. It is instructive to compare the late Renaissance organ at Oosthuizen (*c.* 1520) and the organ at Noordbroek (Arp Schnitger, 1698), which has a mid-baroque case. It will be seen that the same considerations dictated the interior design and dimensions of each case: the height of the pipes of the basic stop, the scales, and the disposition of the whole division.

With the typical Schnitger instrument, each division was designed to be tonally complete within itself, making coupling never absolutely necessary and rarely desirable, although always possible, because of the carefully balanced leverage in the action. This was attested to by 18th-century players of the Zwolle organ.[12] Because of the lack of need to couple, the fact that the sound came from a different height for each division was a musical advantage; each division (with its own individual pitch level and character)

---

[11]Perhaps this balance to a nicety between artistic and practical requirements is characteristic of a masterpiece. Bach wrote many of his cantatas with ceremonial events in mind; in the same way organ builders produced works of art from which the practical requirements did not detract. Just as the case achieved its form for both artistic and practical reasons, so both musical and physical demands of the key action gave the organ its symmetric and logical chest disposition: main division and Brust tiered in front of the player, Rückpositiv behind, and Pedal divided on either side.

[12]Joachim Hess wrote in 1774 that one of the most impressive features of this organ was its light action: "That with all four keyboards coupled together, it was so easy to play." He also mentioned a tremulant, affecting the whole organ, the speed of which could be regulated by a "remarkable drawknob" (Trekker). Hess, *Disposition der merkwaardigste kerkorgelen.*

was associated with a certain location, and the player or composer could utilize this for contrast. All of the organ's sounds came from the same direction, which obviated the disrupting effect common in many modern electric organs, when divisions are to the left and right, fore, aft, and above—for reasons more of expediency than of music.

2. *Actions*. Slider chest and mechanical action were used in preference to other possible chest and key actions then available (such as the *springlade*). This combination is superior for several reasons:

a. It gives the player control over the speed of the opening of the pallet, with consequent influence over attack. Real articulation thus becomes possible. This is especially true of the Brustwerk, and of any other division which is located very close to the keys. The advantage is a subtle one, often not immediately apparent to the player. But the aural difference, though perhaps slight for one note or chord, has a cumulative effect, especially in defining the difference between very legato and very detached playing. On a well-balanced action, a chord struck with force has a more incisive attack than a chord for which the keys are depressed gently.

b. The tone channel in the chest enhances both unanimity of speech and blend of the sound of two or more pipes, because all the pipes for one note receive their wind from the same channel.

c. The long pallet and tone channel have a cushioning effect on the entry of the air into the pipes, producing a distinct and characteristic attack not obtainable as yet with any other system.

d. Perhaps most important of all, the player can *feel* the action through the key, and he thus feels that he is more in control of the instrument, with the result that he plays with greater security and sensitivity. Therefore, the organ *sounds* better, and this in turn helps the performer to play even more accurately and expressively.[13] The first reaction of the player is likely to be a critical one, merely because the "feel" is different from an electric action. However, continued experience with a mechanical action gives the sensitive player results which are not obtainable with an electric chest and key action.

---

[13]This is discussed by D. A. Flentrop in two articles entitled "Organ Building in Europe" (*The Diapason*, November and December, 1956).

e. This action not only permits but requires the location of the keyboards within the instrument (as with all other keyboard instruments), rather than outside of it as a remote-control division.

3. *Disposition.* These organs had a disposition related to the case and to the size and acoustics of the building as well as to the resources of the instrument itself and the space available for it. Pipes were not mitered. This disposition did not vary from the basic practice of founding each division on a Principal stop— usually called "Prestant," when it was displayed in the case front— of appropriate pitch. A complete disposition would have a complete Principal chorus and a smaller flute chorus, with relatively few reeds (except in the Pedal, where reeds were considered more important); these were also related in scale and intensity to the pitch and scale of the Prestant. If the basic Prestant was of 8′ pitch, the disposition would normally include 8′, 4′, 2⅔′, 2′, and a mixture of 1⅓′ pitch. A flute chorus was begun on each division when possible, usually going through 8′, 4′, 2′, with a 16′ (often a Quintadena, but not always) appearing on the main division. Reeds were considered essential in the Pedal, especially at 16′ pitch —full-length, if possible—and an 8′ full-length Trumpet was customary on the main division, with each division having at least one reed. These encompassed a great variety of pipe shapes, pitch, and quality.

The term "Prestant," used here after the northern European custom, is an example of the care with which early builders named the various registers. It refers to the basic rank of Principal tone, which stands in the front of the case, receiving its wind from the same chest as the other pipes. Thus, this term, in its most accurate application, does not refer to a specific voice of given pitch and quality (as it was later used in France by Cavaillé-Coll to designate a 4′ Principal of rather narrow scale); it might refer to 32′, 16′, 8′, 4′, or 2′ pitch, depending on the basic pitch of the division for which it is the "Prestant" (from the Latin *praestare,* to stand in front). Prestant pipes are not for decoration, although they make a handsome façade, but being the most important pipes within a division of the organ, they are naturally given the most prominent location. The Prestants cause the organ to look like what it really is, since case height is always dictated by the length of the longest Prestant pipe.

The mixture pitches of the different divisions were a critical factor in giving each division a special character related to the basic pitch level. Hence, in contrast to the main division mixture (called "Mixtuur") of 1⅓', the Positiv mixture (called "Scherp" in Dutch and "Scharff" in German) was likely to be of ⅔', and the Brust of ⅓' (usually a "Cimbel"). Only when there was more than one mixture on a division was there any likelihood of repeating the basic pitch on another keyboard; an exception to this was the pitch of Schnitger's Pedal "Mixtuur," which had both the same name and the same pitch (1⅓') as the main division. The organ at Zwolle is a good example of this scheme carried to its fullest proportions.

4. *Acoustics.* The Zwolle organ is housed in a very resonant building (about 6 seconds when empty, 3 seconds when filled with people), and it is placed free-standing in the west gallery, the usual location for organs, especially large ones. Very few organs, except single-keyboard "house" (cabinet) instruments, were used in small buildings or spaces of less than 100,000 cubic feet. Larger buildings were usually made of masonry with wooden vaulted roofs, and there were significant acoustical benefits often lacking nowadays.

Although full treatment of placement and resonance is beyond the scope of this discussion, they are of critical importance, and cannot be ignored or left to the whim of an architect, who is likely to consider a "dead" room the ideal acoustical situation, with the organ conveniently out of sight. It is impossible to have a completely successful organ in a dead building, because the organ *and* building, not the organ alone, make the sound. About 3 seconds resonance, when the building was *filled,* was characteristic of the Schnitger instruments. Their effectiveness would doubtless be seriously weakened by an "acousticized" hall.

5. *Scales* were always related to the "basic" (Prestant) stop, which in turn was related to the acoustics and size of the building. Furthermore, scales varied considerably among different Schnitger instruments, depending on the acoustical conditions, so that copies of these scales in a modern instrument in a different environment might make no sense at all. This explains the failure of recent attempts to transfer so-called "18th-century scales" to new instruments; without the appropriate case, voicing, action, etc., such an

instrument would be doomed in advance.

6. *Voicing* was invariably as uncomplicated as possible, with virtually no nicking and with completely open foot-holes. Loudness was regulated *not* at the foot of the pipe, but at the languid and lower lip; the difference in loudness between flue registers (flutes or Principals) was very small. Intensity resulted not from "loud" stops but from the total sound, comprising the blended sound of ranks of different pitches coming from a common chest and resonating case.

Wooden pipes were seldom used, even for flutes; high percentage tin was preferred for Principals. There are no wooden pipes at all in the organs at Zwolle, Steinkirchen, and Noordbroek.[14]

Although a pronounced attack noise or "chiff" was characteristic of some flue registers, it did not occur in most of the voicing; and it was less frequent in Schnitger's work than in many "neobaroque" organs made by modern builders in connection with the "organ reform" of recent years.

Wind supply was no obstacle for Schnitger; it was adequate and steady enough to meet any legitimate musical demands, including coupling. This will be clear to anyone who plays the organ at Zwolle, with its twelve formidable bellows placed there by the Schnitgers in 1721—and still in use, electrically driven. Wind pressures in this organ are 3.38″ for manuals, and 3.9″ for Pedal (water gauge).

A very important and usually neglected aspect of the matter of wind stability is the influence exerted by one pipe upon another pipe sounding at the same time or immediately afterwards. There is no musical objection to slight momentary variations in wind supply; on the contrary, the cross-influence upon the speech of pipes sounded simultaneously or one after the other constitutes an expressive factor which is desirable in some music. This is especially true in the case of small instruments, which lose part of

---

[14]Schnitger's instruments always had a generous supply of flute stops, with as much variety as possible—Rohrflutes, Gedeckts, Spitzflutes, Nachthorns, etc.—each name being associated with a specific pipe shape. There were also Quintadenas, but these were rarely, if ever, the only 8′ flute on a division; their sound was apparently considered too thin or "quinty" to be used as the basis for a chorus. They were accompanied by another 8′ flute on the same division, and never appeared at 16′ pitch in the Pedal.

their character and flexibility when the wind pressure is rigidly unshakable just for the sake of being unshakable. In addition, where voicing is concerned, many fine 17- and 18th-century instruments derive part of their appeal from the fact that many registers are not intended to be absolutely smooth and even, with each note a carbon copy of the other. This has a significant relation to the wind supply, since some registers (especially flutes) may get a quality of dullness or sameness if the wind supply is entirely rigid and the voicing "smooth," in the 19th-century "English" manner.

It should be emphasized that the foregoing characteristics of Schnitger organs are all equally important. It would be useless to concentrate on one or two to the exclusion of the others.

To summarize, these are the factors which the Schnitger tradition considered of the utmost importance:

1. Each division of the organ in its own free-standing case of appropriate dimensions in relation to its basic Prestant pitch and to the other divisions of the organ.

2. A light, responsive mechanical key action, with a slider stop action.

3. Disposition related in both pitch and scale to the basic Prestant displayed in the case front.

4. Live acoustics, with a resonance period of at least three seconds when the building was filled.

5. Variable scales.

6. Low wind pressures, and voicing with wide-open foot holes without nicking.

MUSIC AND HISTORY

THE ORGAN plays a historical repertoire, and demands a historical approach. The instrument has a clearly documented development; in each of several periods and styles, masterpieces were
produced. The highly refined examples of the organ builder's art
and craft demonstrate unmistakably that the builders had clear
concepts of what an organ should be—what it should look like
and sound like, and how it should be used by the player. Although
each of these periods and styles produced examples of classic
stature, it is not true that each style evolved into something either
new or better. Rather, each was in itself an expression of an artistic
ideal, and can be judged only in terms of the context and artistic
aims of its own time and place. In relation to these classic instruments, and to the idea of the organ as an instrument with in-
violable, inherent form possessing certain limitations, organ building began to deteriorate as early as the middle of the 18th century.
This can be seen even in the work of the Silbermanns before 1750.[1]

A historical orientation is thus essential, for player, composer,
builder, and listener, in the interest not of academic antiquarianism but of music. If the historical sense is ignored or consulted
only when convenient—which is frequently the case when a builder attaches himself to superficial aspects of one particular style—
the result is a nonentity. Stylistic integrity, which requires an
artistically disciplined and historically informed comprehension
of the nature of the instrument and its music, gives way to a formless eclecticism.

---

[1]For example, in the Ebersmunster organ (1730), while the Positiv remains
intact tonally, there is no Pedal case; there is less "traditional" (in terms
of Schnitger) contrast in mixture pitches between the keyboards; and there
is no mixture at all on the Pedal, which is already losing its contrapuntal
and independent solo function.

Limitations Give Identity

Both the instrument and the music which has been composed for it have inherent limitations. The organ will not play certain styles of composition well, and certain textures and techniques do not sound well when performed on it, because they do not suit its nature. These limitations, far from detracting, help to give identity and character. With the organ more than any other instrument, to divorce musical from historical understanding is to forfeit its highest artistic potential.

Creativity and Imitation

One obvious danger is the risk of subjecting music or an instrument to an analysis of merely mathematical proportions. Inflexible rules have not usually been compatible with art, and a creative perspective is essential. Uncritical imitation—by the performer or the instrument maker—can hardly be an artistic endeavor. The more subtle task is to retain an awareness of historical practices and ideas without just copying the work of earlier masters.

This problem is important for the player and builder because one of the loudest (albeit uninformed) criticisms is that an organ embodying essential historical principles is merely antiquarian and not relevant to the musical life of the present day. This need not be so if the aim behind the instrument is a musical one: to bring to life important music of whatever period, music which has as much artistic vitality now as ever.

Musically Authentic Performance

The musical aim is to do justice to the intentions of the composer. Ideally this means that the sounds which were available to the composer must be available to the present-day performer. But it is not possible to have a completely "authentic" performance of most music of the 17th and 18th centuries without going to far greater lengths than present-day performers have thought feasible.

The ideal solution would be, first, to have the original instrument in its original condition in its original acoustical environment; and second, to have a player with perfect knowledge of performance practices when the organ was built. The former is occasionally possible with the organ or harpsichord, but it is rare.

It is not only the instrument itself that is problematical. With concerted music, problems of historical accuracy multiply: the substitution of women's voices for boys', the great variety of wind instruments, the differences in sound and structure of stringed instruments and their bows. To duplicate an acoustical setting which is particularly critical for the organ would be a formidable task. And yet, the style and spirit of the music must not be compromised in the attempt to provide for technical details—the hardest problem of all to solve with artistic poise. In view of such obstacles, it seems unrealistic to expect complete authenticity.

The problem of authenticity and its relation to artistic integrity is largely one of our own day. Only recently have technological advances in printing and other communications media made the music of the past available throughout the world. Musicians now have at their disposal not just what is contemporary or local, but a large part of the important music created over four or more centuries. With the rediscovery of this wealth of music from the past, and because of its great artistic merit, there may be a temptation to de-emphasize the contemporary in favor of the antique. This is particularly true of the organ, since the bulk of its repertoire comes from the period before 1750. No responsible musician is in favor of ignoring present-day musical composition. On the other hand, earlier music must not be denied its right to performance so long as it really has something to say to us—and the organ music of the 17th and 18th centuries certainly does.

Just as the harpsichord music of Bach, Couperin, Scarlatti, and others has brought us back to the harpsichord, so we must return to an appropriate medium for the organ repertoire.[2] Players

---

[2]In this connection Paul Hindemith writes: "All the traits that made music of the past lovable to its contemporary performers and listeners were inextricably associated with the kind of sound then known and appreciated. If we replace this sound by the sounds typical of our modern instruments and their treatment, we are counterfeiting the musical message the original sound was supposed to transmit. Consequently, all music ought to be per-

who are seriously concerned with the articulation and style of the music will no longer be satisfied with an instrument lacking the proper resources of sound, character, and action.[3]

The Player a Specialist

For most instruments, the player finds it impractical nowadays, if not impossible, to assimilate all of the techniques and styles from many different composers and periods. He is often forced to specialize in one genre, still trying to retain awareness of the merits and nature of the music beyond his performing scope. This need not be a disadvantage for the organist, because he plays a historical instrument which draws its most significant repertoire from a few highly perfected styles, an instrument which is idiomatically suited to these styles and not always to others. It is at this point that the historical awareness of the builder and the player again becomes essential. "Jot and tittle" imitation becomes irrelevant when one understands the stylistic principles underlying the instrument and the music, because both are founded on freedom within limitations —a basic artistic principle wherever form is concerned. These limitations, as we shall see, result in performance which is true to the composer's intentions, and artistically alive rather than academic.

---

formed with the means of production that were in use when the composer gave it to his contemporaries." *A Composer's World* (Harvard University Press, 1952), p. 167.

[3]Wilfrid Mellers, reviewing recordings of Couperin's *Leçons des Ténèbres,* notes: "If we attempt now to perform Couperin—or for that matter Bach —with some respect for the conventions within which he worked, the reason is not basically antiquarian: it is because, so performed, the music makes better sense to us in the 20th century." He goes on to say that "interpreted non-historically, Couperin's *Leçons* make no sense at all; whereas re-created with humility they speak to us with immediate poignancy." *Musical Quarterly,* January, 1956, p. 120.

HISTORICAL INSTRUMENT: HISTORICAL REPERTOIRE

IN PAST times the organ reached a very high stage of refinement; as with the harpsichord, its nature was clearly understood and its form superbly defined. It was associated with an unequalled repertoire and the conventions for its performance. An important part of the contemporary musician's responsibility to future excellence is a mature understanding of what has been achieved in the past.

The writer believes that the organs of the Schnitgers and the music of Bach form a perfect combination: an ideal instrument suited to the performance of a great repertoire. In the following discussion, this combination will be referred to as a norm.

Confusing Terms

Despite its vogue, the term "baroque" is an inadequate one when applied to the organ. It has come to mean different things to different people (especially in the United States), and it sometimes implies an antiquarian approach. Therefore, the term "Bach-Schnitger norm" is proposed because it facilitates documentation of both repertoire and instruments involved. It is specific and less subject to ambiguous interpretation. The word "baroque" has recently been applied to instruments lacking some of the characteristics which in terms of the Schnitger tradition would allow them to be distinctly identified as organs.

In using the work of the Schnitgers as a standard of comparison, it must be remembered that many valid instruments which preceded and came after them did not conform in detail to the Schnitger scheme. But the basic principles underlying the design of all these instruments are similar. There is consistent attention to action, chest, case, scaling, voicing, relative location of divisions, disposition, and acoustics.

The instruments of different composers in northern and southern Europe between 1600 and 1750 differed more in resource than in quality of sound. An organ ideally suited to Bach will probably not render Sweelinck's music with complete authenticity. The same holds true for other composers and styles. The selection of the Bach-Schnitger organ as a norm is musically defensible, in view of the fact that Bach, his contemporaries, and his immediate predecessors produced a great amount of organ music of very high quality. By singular good fortune, the Schnitgers worked at the end of a period when more significant composers wrote for the organ than ever before or since; and it was during this same period that craftsmen of a high order were engaged in organ building.

Inter-influence of Instrument and Repertoire

Between 1600 and 1750 there was a reciprocal influence between the organ itself and the music composed for it. Both achieved a high degree of refinement simultaneously. Thus, Bach's music seems to spring to life and sound "convincing" on a Schnitger instrument; and by the same token the Schnitger organ makes sense when it is heard playing the music of Bach. Difficulties are encountered when unsuitable music is performed on such an instrument, just as the works of Bach lose much of their effectiveness on an eclectic modern electric-action organ.

Idiomatic Style

What was the style of musical composition which fitted so well the instrument contemporary with it? Diversity was part of the genius of this style, and generalizations about it cannot replace close study of the music itself or documentary information about the conventions of performance. However, there are three characteristic techniques which can be mentioned. While first respecting the idiomatic requirements of the keyboard and the sonorities and textures appropriate to the organ, this music is predominantly based on (1) counterpoint, (2) "terraced dynamic" chordal and running passages, and (3) the ornamented aria (that is, intricate melodic writing with accompaniment).

These techniques of counterpoint, terraced dynamic, and aria were admirably suited to the nature of the organ. Consequently, they were developed to an impressive degree by Bach and others who sensed and accepted the styles of writing which would make the organ most successful as a musical medium. At the same time, it was for music with these stylistic and idiomatic characteristics that the Schnitgers made their organs. Only slightly later, even in instruments of great beauty made by Silbermann or Müller,[1] one begins to experience difficulty in registrating the Bach repertoire. The decadence in design had begun.

Which Organ Is Most Useful?

If a builder begins with a musical point of departure, he is forced to choose what repertoire the organ is to play, and then decide how to design the organ tonally—and still, the identity of the organ itself as a musical medium must not be violated.[2] The Schnitger organ was not made for César Franck and will not render his music authentically; the mixtures are higher than those of the 19th-century French instrument, there are no Celestes or swell boxes, scales are radically different, reeds are less frequent and of different timbre. Franck did not compose his music for a Schnitger instrument. Bach is never performed with complete success on a Cavaillé-Coll organ for precisely the same reason: either the builder did not have this music in mind, or he misunderstood it as far as authentic performance is concerned.

If authentic performance is desired (of even the most frequently performed segments of the repertoire) a decision must be made between music written before 1750 and late 19th-century music, mostly French. One instrument will perhaps render both the 18th- and the 19th-century music in an artistically interesting way (and this is simplifying the matter), but the performance will not be authentic as far as the specific intentions of the composer go.

---

[1]For example, the organs at Marmoutier (Silbermann, 1710) and Beverwijk (Müller, 1756).

[2]For a lucid discussion of this question, see Erich Goldschmidt, "Problems of Contemporary Organ Building," *Organ Institute Quarterly*, Vol. VIII, No. 2 (1955), pp. 15 ff.

However, an organ of the Schnitger type will be musically effective for much of the best 19th- and 20th-century music,[3] whereas a less well-designed modern electric-action or "all-purpose" organ—or even a Cavaillé-Coll—will not be effective for the music of Bach and his predecessors. Finally, the player is forced to make some value judgments about his repertoire, and these judgments are facilitated by an accurate knowledge of what his instrument really is—or should be.

The Contemporary Composer

The more musically ideal the organ, the more genuine interest composers seem to evince. The modern electric-action organ is as far from the instrument of Franck as from that of Bach.[4] One has only to play Franck on a Cavaillé-Coll (such as the one at Ste. Clothilde) or on other organs in the 19th-century French style to see that similar names on stop knobs do not denote similar sounds, especially in American dry acoustics. Consequently, the present-day composer does not know exactly what sort of instrument he is writing for; therefore, he usually does not write for the organ. Especially in the United States, there is a variety of instruments which are not within the limits of a well-defined style. They have no consistent elements of design related both to repertoire and to a valid concept of the instrument. The result is very little recent organ music of high caliber.

The reader must be reminded that this is a formidable artistic

---

[3]See recorded works of Alain and Messiaen, played on the Schnitger organ at Alkmaar by Piet Kee (Dutch HMV 7 EPH 1005), or the performance of Messiaen by Robert Noehren on the Moreau organ at Gouda (Allegro Elite Recordings). This question is discussed in Bornefeld, *Orgelbau und neue Orgelmusik*, p. 16.

[4]The "all-purpose" idea in design is a pitfall avoided in many modern European instruments, even though they may not be in the Schnitger style. An example is the organ in St. Benigue Cathedral, Dijon; originally built by Riepp (1740-1743), it has now been completely rebuilt and modernized by Roethinger (Strasbourg, 1953-1955), partly on the advice of Marcel Dupré. It retains only the chests of the original organ together with some of the pipes, and is twenty stops larger. It is in fact a modern, authentically "French" organ, reminiscent of Cavaillé-Coll; but in sound it does not closely resemble the "French" division of an American organ.

Renaissance Choir Organ:

I   Alkmaar, Grote Kerk, Jan van Kovelen, 1511.

Restored, H. W. Flentrop, 1939.

Renaissance Choir Organ:

II Amsterdam, Nieuwe Kerk. Jan Zwart, *c.* 1550.
Restored, D. A. Flentrop, 1947. Temporarily dismantled.

III Cappel. Arp Schnitger, 1679.

IV   Steinkirchen. Arp Schnitger, 1687.
Restored, Rudolph von Beckerath,   1955.

V   Mexico City, Cathedral. Unknown Spanish builder, *c.* 1688 - 1696.

VI   Noordbroek, Grote Kerk. Arp Schnitger, 1698.

VII   Marmoutier, Abby. Johann Andreas Silbermann. 1710.
Restored, Mühleisen, 1955.

VIII   Cabinet Organ by John Snetzler, London, *c.* 1748.
Owned by Colonial Williamsburg, Virginia. Now dismantled.

IX   Beverwijk, Grote Kerk. Christian Müller, 1756.
       Restored, H. W. Flentrop, 1936.

X/XI   A Cabinet Organ: Naarden, Vituskerk.   J. Strümphler, 1781

Restored, D. A. Flentrop, 1951. Now owned by the Netherlands Bach Society.

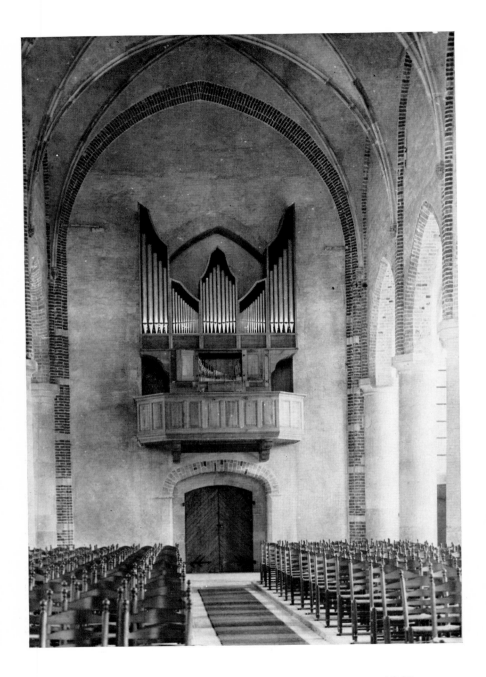

XII   Groenlo, Grote Kerk. D. A. Flentrop, 1952.

XIII   Rotterdam, Paaskerk. D. A. Flentrop, 1953.

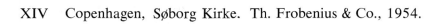

XIV   Copenhagen, Søborg Kirke. Th. Frobenius & Co., 1954.

XV   Cleveland, Ohio, Trinity Lutheran Church. Rudolph von Beckerath,
      1957.

XVI   Busch-Reisinger Museum, Harvard University. D. A. Flentrop, 1958.

XVII   Beuel-Vilich, Pfarrkirche St. Peter.
Rieger-Orgelbau (designed by Josef von Glatter-Götz), 1959.

Case

XVIII/XIX   Baltimore, Maryland, Mount Calvary Episcopal Church.

Key desk

Andover Organ Company (designed by Charles Fisk), 1961.

XX Augsburg, Barfüsserkirche. Rieger-Orgelbau (designed by Josef von Glatter-Götz), 1958.

problem about which it is easy to be superficial or make glib generalities. "Idiomatic," "musical," and "authentic" are not the only relevant terms in judging the expressive or aesthetic qualities of music. And no artistic purpose is served by worshipping one particular instrument or style and denying that others are valid. The root of the dilemma for both organ builders and players is the frequent lack of a coherent concept of the instrument's nature and of the characteristics which made various earlier organs great. Confusion or reluctance to investigate acknowledged masterpieces of earlier builders has led to a formless eclecticism which robs many modern instruments of character. Some of these are only "imitations" of organs, analogous to the uninformed work of a commercial architect, vaguely called "Colonial" but having no style of its own and no relation to the style it purports to be inspired by.[5]

This is not to say that changes in organ design cannot be made in an artistic way. But one cannot intelligently alter the model until he comprehends it for what it really is.

Concerning 19th-century organ music, it is worth pointing out that composers like Brahms and Mendelssohn had available mechanical-action organs much more similar to those of Bach than to electric-action instruments with eclectic dispositions. There is little justification for the often heard "romanticized" registration used in the works of these composers, in view of the organs for which they wrote.

Returning to the Schnitger tradition, why is it that a late 17th- or early 18th-century organ will play music (if not absolutely authentically, at least musically) written much later? First, an organ which is a valid musical medium is likely to render musically a repertoire which is written in an idiomatic style; as long as the basic design has integrity, the difference in specific sound is not so critical. Second, from an idiomatic standpoint, the music of

---

[5]In the present day, the idea of style per se often gets lost in an effort to imitate some earlier style or to be fashionable. Geoffrey Scott speaks of the problem of "style rather than a sequence of styles," maintaining that, beginning in the 19th century, we have become concerned not with the concept of style itself in art but with trying to reconstruct or copy various styles of the past, often without being aware of the context in which they were originally produced. Scott, *The Architecture of Humanism* (New York, Scribner's, 1924), pp. 127 ff.

a composer like Franck is less specifically organ music, and at times even less specifically keyboard music. Thus, it suffers less when detached from its original specific sound and transposed for another instrument than does music (such as Buxtehude's) which demands the appropriate instrument and acoustics, not just for a musical rendering, but even for an intelligible one.[6]

Incompatible Music

Why this seemingly great incompatibility between music of different periods, especially in regard to authenticity of performance? And why does some music (such as that of Pachelbel or Buxtehude) suffer more when not given an authentic rendition? As already indicated, decadence in both organ building and writing for the organ began in the mid-18th century. What came later is distortion, encouraged by a shift of interest to the piano, the orchestra, and romantic opera.

The Organ and Its Limitations

The nature of the instrument cannot be changed to suit the style of a given composer or the whims of a particular builder— not even the brilliant experiments of Cavaillé-Coll. To date no

---

[6]The dependence of Buxtehude and similar stylists on the appropriate instrument may be seen in his *Passacaglia* in D minor: the piece is in four clearly defined sections, with obvious requirements to shift keyboards after each; there is a minimum of time permitted to change stops. Such a work fails to make complete sense on a modern electric-action organ, where the performer must usually make changes of stops within one division of the organ, rather than shift to a new division in each instance. Also, the appropriate *location* of Brust, Hauptwerk, Positiv, etc., contributes greatly to the success of Buxtehude's piece. Another example of the affinity of the music for the instrument is Bach's *Passacaglia,* especially in measures 162 ff., where the addition of a fifth voice arouses great excitement in intensity and volume; on the right instrument, this obviates the necessity to add a register, for which there is no rhythmic provision. This subtle and exciting event goes unheard on a badly designed organ in a dead hall; or else the player tries to make a change of registration, which destroys either the rhythm or the phrasing.

composer or builder has appeared—with the possible exception of Franck—who can disregard or successfully transcend the limitations imposed by the nature of the organ. As Stravinsky has observed: "Which of us has ever heard talk of art as other than a realm of freedom? This sort of heresy is uniformly widespread because it is imagined that art is outside the bounds of ordinary activity. . . . The more constraints one imposes, the more one frees oneself of the chains that shackle the spirit."[7]

Finally, there have been virtually no really significant advances, related to a valid repertoire, in the development of the organ in the last 100 years.[8]

What, then, should be done when a new organ is to be designed for use in a contemporary situation? For an artistically defensible instrument, we must build in accordance with the same principles which were observed by the best designers who worked during the golden age of organ building. Players must submit, just as they do with the violin, the piano, and other instruments, to the limitations imposed by the nature of the organ.

What if the new instrument is less comfortable to play than a modern electric-action instrument, with its detached console, many pistons and other mechanical conveniences? If artistic aims are put first, then some of the props which inhibit them must be relinquished. In the last analysis, they impair the musical qualities of the instrument and hamstring the performer. They remove him one step further from the music. Comfort in manipulating a machine does not compensate for loss of artistic control. And

---

[7]Igor Stravinsky, *Poetics of Music* (Harvard University Press, 1946) pp. 64, 65. The same idea is also mentioned by the Danish builder Frobenius in a pamphlet, "Demonstration of the Frobenius Organ in Søborg Kirke, Copenhagen" (1955, Frobenius Orgelbyggeri, Lyngby, Denmark), and by D. A. Flentrop in his article "Organ Building in Europe," *The Diapason*, November, 1956.

[8]For instance, Ernest Skinner's many tonal adaptations (English Horn, French Horn, Erzähler) either represented new names for basically old voices, or were orchestral in quality (and thus detached from the organ repertoire), or did not fit coherently into the flue ensemble required by the music. The Celeste, while not a 19th-century invention—it appeared at least as early as the 18th—might be considered justified by the 19th-century repertoire, since it is called for by such composers as Franck in registrations specified for a given work *(Chorale in E)*.

most of the mechanical devices to which the American player
is conditioned also tend to obscure the logical functions of the
independent divisions of the organ—partly because he depends
too much on coupling individual registers between manuals—
and to encourage unmusical changes of register, because he can
do it with such ease.

As previously noted, the location and scaling of the divisions
of an organ in relation to each other is of great musical significance.
"Rückpositiv" denotes a division of specific disposition, scaling,
and position. Simply to mark stop knobs "Positiv" (while the pipes
might be in a swell box located behind another division of the
organ, or even in another section of the building) does not assure
their artistic usefulness in playing the repertoire.

6 THE IDEAL AND THE COMPROMISE

"In order to achieve the right relative, we must understand the ideal."[1] If one compares a mediocre instrument with a more ideal one, the individual differences may not appear striking. Some of the characteristics which make a work of art worthy of its name are necessarily subtle ones; differences of voicing, disposition, acoustics, action, case, relative location of divisions— these may appear slight in themselves. But if differences between the mediocre and the ideal are subtle, they are nonetheless of critical importance. The craftsman is often accused by the dilettante of splitting hairs; but if he deserves the name of artist, it is part of his vocation to split hairs.[2] An ideal musical instrument, just like a painting or a design for a building, is by its very nature a perfectionist's undertaking.

Although the ideal may be only approximated, even this accomplishment will lose its meaning if perfection is not kept constantly in mind. If the ideal is temporarily shelved, then there remains not compromise, which implies awareness of the ideal, but expediency, which is beyond the realm of art.

Identifying a Masterpiece

A constant problem is the attempt by inexperienced persons to "improve" a masterpiece, usually by "modernizing" it with

---

[1] S. Bixler, *Terry Lectures* (Yale University Press, 1946).

[2] Dorothy Sayers pinpoints the artistic perspective by saying, "It is the duty of the worker not to serve the public but to serve the work"; otherwise he may end up merely trying to make money, to become famous, or to please everybody in general, and forget the standard which only he can set for himself. Dorothy L. Sayers, "Why Work?" in *Creed or Chaos* (London, Methuen, 1954), pp. 61 ff.

little regard for its original identity. This only indicates an inability to recognize a masterpiece in the first place. It is just as important to be on guard against being exclusively modern as it is to be on guard against being exclusively antiquarian. In classic examples of craftsmanship—a well-preserved Schnitger organ, a Ruckers harpsichord, or a Stradivarius violin—one does well to comprehend the excellence attained by the original builder, without presuming to improve upon it.

The same holds true for those performers who insist on prophesying in reverse that Bach and his contemporaries would have made certain uses of new tonal or expressive resources now available.[3] It is more likely that Bach would have written something entirely different from fugues and the Brandenburg Concerti.

The important point for the organist and organ builder is that each modernization of the instrument or the music may remove us one step further from the intentions of the composer and the essence of the style. Again, the razor's edge which separates imitation from informed creativity is a sharp one, and the freedom within limits due the performer or instrument maker can only be used fully when he both feels *and* knows. While the music of a composer of the first rank may transcend the most abysmal performances on the most inadequate instruments, it achieves its truest expression only with the appropriate tonal resources, methods of control (action), and style of playing.

---

[3] A letter to Mendelssohn from his father notes: "A question is not infrequently raised as to whether Handel, if he had written in our day, would have made use of all the existing musical facilities in composing his oratorios, which in fact only means: would the wonted artistic form to which we give the name of Handel assume the same shape now that it did a hundred years ago . . . the question however, ought to be put in a different form: not whether Handel would have composed his oratorios now as he did a century ago, but rather, whether he would have composed oratorios at all. Hardly—if they had to be written in the style of those of today." Felix Mendelssohn, *Letters* (New York, Pantheon, 1945), p. 240.

Ralph Kirkpatrick touches on the same question and reaches the same conclusion in his preface to the *Goldberg Variations* (New York, G. Schirmer, 1938), p. ix.

Musical Sound and Music

Especially because the organ comprises such a large collection of different sounds, one must keep in mind that a "pleasant" sound is not always musically useful. Some sounds which are appropriate for one style or texture are drawbacks for the adequate realization of another. Yet the uninformed design of many organs gives them resources which are as bizarrely out of place for the repertoire as a lute might be for Beethoven or a harpsichord for Chopin.

Organ sounds are important not only in themselves, but also in their relation to the ensemble of their division as a whole, and to the repertoire which the organ is to play. A stop of fascinating timbre might be musically useless in relation to other sounds of the organ or to the music. The fact that this has been ignored helps to account for the total loss of identity which the organ suffered during the 19th century. The cinema organ of the 1920's exhibited the grotesque proportions which were ultimately reached.

Style and Repertoire

The musical significance of the several historical types of organs depends on their stylistic coherence as a medium, and on the musical validity of the repertoire to be played on them. The organ style of Schnitger is intimately connected with northern European music from about 1675 to 1735, the style of Clicquot with mid-18th-century French music, Antegnati with Frescobaldi, and Nijhof with Sweelinck.[4]

This consists in deciding whether an organ will sound musically effective (1) when it is played as its builder designed it to be played, in accordance with his principles of registration, and (2) when the repertoire for which it was designed is played with appropriate stylistic technique.

---

[4]The Antegnati family were the leading organ builders of 17th-century Italy. Nijhof built the organ used by Sweelinck in the Oude Kerk, Amsterdam; it was replaced in 1726 by the present organ (by J. C. Müller), which has since been much altered.

Judging an Organ

There is no point in judging Bach's music in terms of Brahms's, and there is no point in judging an organ intended to play Bach's music in terms of an organ intended for another kind of repertoire. Many of the most notable English organs, designed primarily to accompany the Anglican service, are inadequate for the performance of Bach. The influence of these organs on American instruments has been enormous almost to the present day, contributing to the confusing eclecticism of much organ design in the United States.

An organ intended for a given repertoire must be played with careful consideration for the registration practices related to the organ's disposition. Schnitger thought in terms of distinct divisions, each based on a Principal rank of a certain pitch, crowned with a mixture; his instruments must be played with the appropriate registration and articulation, or they lose their identity as a logical and effective medium.[5]

When Is a Historical Organ Musically Important?

An instrument of historical interest must be associated with enough significant music to make it worth investigating in relation to present-day performance. There are other important matters which bear on its musical worth:

(1) There is a difference between restoring and rebuilding an old organ. Virtually no 18th-century instruments remain which have not had extensive repairs—either sympathetic or otherwise. An organ may have lost part or all of the character invested in it by the original builder.

(2) A great many old instruments have in fact been altered, often under the guise of restoration; some no longer sound the

---

[5]There is frequently a tendency to judge an organ in terms of its ability to accompany congregational singing. In reality, any well-made, well-placed organ in good acoustical surroundings can satisfy this simple but important requirement. However, an organ might be able to do this and still fall far short of playing its legitimate repertoire adequately.

way they did when important music was written for them. One such instrument, still of great interest, can be seen in the Bavokerk in Haarlem, the Netherlands. This organ, like many of its contemporaries, underwent changes during the 19th century which were quite alien to the intentions of Müller, its builder.[6] Often an organ has gone through several complete renovations, still retaining its original case; an example is the instrument in the Grote Kerk in Alkmaar. First built in the style of the early 17th century without an independent Pedal, this organ was given a second (but equally valid) form by the Schnitgers in 1725.

---

[6]It was restored in 1961 by the firm of Marcussen (Abenraa, Denmark).

EXCELLENCE in a musical instrument depends on a group of extremely subtle qualities which may not even be noticeable when taken singly, but which make all the difference when taken as a whole; the degree of excellence is directly proportional to the degree of care expended on these details.

When a Bach piece which was written for a recorder is performed on a Boehm system silver flute, the discerning and knowledgeable listener will notice that, regardless of the player's virtuosity, the music fails to convey the unvarnished intentions of the composer. This is not only because the sound is different, but also because the player is compelled to play differently. His instrument may not have the limitations of the recorder, and superficially this may seem to be an advantage; however, it has other limitations, which reduce its ability to play the music of Bach authentically—for instance, an overdeveloped low register, which differs from the sound of the recorder's low register.

Musical performance is like any other art: it is the subtle, distinctive, uncompromising adherence to style and devoted attention to detail which are the stamp of spontaneity and integrity.[1]

---

[1]Eta Harich-Schneider, in *The Harpsichord*, p. 7, speaks of the danger of an extramusical or antiquarian approach to performance. She makes a case for playing music on appropriate instruments: "rather than a romantic yearning for days gone by or because it seems clever or picturesque," the reason is purely musical. "We want to play Baroque music on the Baroque instruments for musical reasons, to keep the music alive, agile, and young. This is best achieved through the medium of the original sound." She says of the antiquarians: "They want the morbid fragrance of the past. By using the old instruments as stage props, for their extra-musical goal, they will finish by abusing the old music itself and turn the whole invaluable treasure of three centuries into façade, masque, costume."

Paradoxically, the two requirements of slider chest and mechanical action in an ideal organ are structurally quite obvious, while their effect on both sound and player is extremely subtle; but the effect is the more important—and the more likely to be overlooked—just because of its subtlety.

The slider chest affects chiefly the *sound* of the organ, because of the blending and the unanimity of speech it allows. With an electric chest this effect is sacrificed, because there is a separate valve for each note.

The mechanical action affects chiefly the *player*, and the way in which he articulates and senses the rhythm of a phrase. It allows him intimate control of the action: as in other keyboard instruments, he *plays* upon the sound-producing mechanism, instead of merely touching an electrical contact as he might touch a doorbell button.

The difference between eclectically designed electric-action organs and instruments by builders like the Schnitgers is greater than between the harpsichord and the piano: while the piano retains its identity as a musical instrument, the "modernized" organ has lost its integrated structure and expressive character.

If the builder or player wishes to bring expressiveness, excitement, spontaneity, and authenticity to the performance of a great repertoire—if his aim is genuinely musical—there must be a wholehearted and candid reinstatement of the basic principles of design as they existed in the golden age of the organ.

PART TWO

REPRESENTATIVE DISPOSITIONS

REPRESENTATIVE dispositions of significant organs, beginning with the late Renaissance, are cited and discussed in the following pages. Comparison of the dispositions with corresponding plates will help in associatng the proportions of the cases with the basic stop of each division, and in understanding the close connection between appearance and resources.

The dispositions and builders have been chosen to help trace the development of the refined styles, which culminated in northern Europe with the instruments of the Schnitger family. It would be an encyclopedic task to cite all of the "significant" instruments. Included here are a minimum of important organs; most of them are now in playable condition and have been responsibly restored; a few have been lost. The majority have been examined by the writer.

Almost all these instruments have been associated with the music of an important composer of the period. The attempt is made to give an example of each major organ-building style of the 17th and 18th centuries, concentrating on the Schnitger work, but pointing out differences in design, especially between northern and southern European instruments.

Comments have been made in regard to the dispositions, in the hope that the reader will follow them in chronological order with due attention to characteristics peculiar to northern or southern instruments. This should make it possible to get a clearer idea of what the Schnitger instruments were like in comparison with those which came before and after. Both large and small organs of the Schnitger family are cited to call attention to the consistency with which they were designed, and to point out that much variety was included in them without violating basic principles.

Later, as can be seen in the disposition of Müller, Andreas Silbermann, and others, fundamental departures from the Schnitger scheme began.

The French instruments, about midway between North and South in design, are good examples of organs related to their contemporary repertoire. The earlier one (St. Gervais) is quite different from the Schnitger work of the same time, especially with regard to the Pedal division, but there are many features appropriate to the music of Couperin. In the later one (Ste. Clothilde), the same kind of relationship to the music of Franck can be seen.

Photographs of several new instruments are included in the text, to indicate the recent appearance in the United States of both imported and domestic mechanical-action organs designed in accordance with many of the basic considerations found in the Schnitger instruments. There is a similar movement in France, led by Norbert Dufourcq, to restore some of the best Couperin-style organs and to consider 18th-century ideas in designing new organs. While the Netherlands has been the leader in definitive restoration, Denmark, Germany, Switzerland, England, and Italy have musicians and builders who are concerned for the preservation of important organs.

Following Part Two is a selective list of recent books and articles, and basic 17th- and 18th-century writings. Although the accuracy of these books is generally commendable, the reader is advised to accept critically information about dispositions, unless details regarding restorations and alterations are included, since an instrument frequently retains only a partial resemblance to the work of the original builder whose name it bears. This is true of some of the Silbermann organs in and around Strasbourg, the organ in the Jakobikirche in Hamburg, in the Oude Kerk, Amsterdam, and many other important instruments. For more extensive information and documentation, the work of careful scholars like Vente and Leonhardt in the Netherlands, Klotz in Germany, Dufourcq and Hardouin in France, and Lunelli in Italy is eminently worth consulting.

But the best procedure is to hear, play, and compare.

1. ALKMAAR, GROTE KERK (Laurenskerk)

Jan van Kovelen, choir organ, 1511; possibly the oldest organ in Europe still in use.[1]

Hoofdwerk

> Doeff 8′ (Principal)
> Holfluijte 8′ (Rohrflute)
> Coppeldoeff 4′ (Principal)
> Baertfluijte 4′
> Gemsenhoern 2′
> Mixtuijre II-III-IV 2′
> Scerp III-IV 1′ (Scharff)
> Trompet 8′

Borstwerk

> Holpijpe 8′
> Fluijte 4' (replaced Kromhoorn, 1625)
> Octaaf 2′
> Schivelet 1′
> Sexquialter II (treble)

Pedaal

> Trompet 8′ (possibly added in the 16th century)

---

[1]Disposition by courtesy of D. A. Flentrop. The organ was restored by his father, H. W. Flentrop, in 1939. There are many very old organs in Europe which have been greatly altered, and it is hard to be certain whether all or part of the pipes, chests, etc., are original. One which the author has not seen, but which is undoubtedly of great interest, is that at Notre Dame de Valère, Sion (Sitten, Switzerland), said to have been built in the late 14th century. See Blanton, "The Oldest Playable Organ...," *The Diapason*, April, 1956, p. 8, and Hardmeyer, *Einführung in die Schweizerische Orgelbaukunst*, p. 11.

2. OOSTHUIZEN, HERVORMDE KERK

Anonymous builder, 1521.[1]
One keyboard.

> Bourdon 8′ (now 16′)
> Praestant 8′
> Octaaf 4′ (2 pipes for each key from A′)
> Quint 2⅔′
> Woudfluit 2′
> Mixtuur II-III 1⅓′
> Sesquialtera II (treble)
> Tremulant

---

[1]Boumann, *Orgels in Nederland*, p. 45. Temporarily dismantled in 1958 because of structural dangers in the church. A restoration is anticipated by the firm of Flentrop.

3. AMSTERDAM, OUDE KERK

Martinus Nijhof (?), 1544-1555; altered 1567-1568; an organ used by Jan Pieterszoon Sweelinck.[1]

Hoofdwerk

Prestant 8′
Prestant 4′ (front pipes)
Roerfluit 8′
Octaaf 2′
Mixtuur
Scherp
Quintadeen 8′
Gemshorn 2′
Tertscymbel
Schalmey 4′
Tremulant

Borst

Roerfluit 4′
Regaal 8′
Kromhoorn 8′

Pedaal

Trompet 8′

Sweelinck (1562-1621), who became municipal organist at the Oude Kerk *c.* 1577, was employed there by the town to play publicly, but not for church services. This was the organ (now lost) used by Sweelinck, and its limited disposition speaks for itself, when his music is considered. The present organ in this church (begun by Christian Vatter in 1726 and completed by Johann Christian Müller in 1739) is a totally different instrument, with many tonal alterations of the 19th century; the action is in very poor condition. A restoration of this organ is expected.

---

[1]Disposition supplied by Gustav Leonhardt, Amsterdam.

4. BRESCIA, SAN GIUSEPPE

Constanzo Antegnati, *c.* 1580.[1]

Principale 16'	Trigesimaterza ⅔'
(diviso in Bassi e Soprani)	Flauto in XV 4'
Ottava 8'	Flauto in XII 5⅓'
Quintadecima 4'	Flauto in VIII 8'
Decimanona 2⅔'	Fiffaro 16'
Vigesimaseconda 2'	PEDALE—Pedalboard only (no stops)
Vigesimasesta 1⅓'	with pull-downs to manual
Vigesimanona 1'	

These four instruments, three of which are still extant, are well worth the close attention of the serious player because of the light they throw on the musical intentions of composers such as Sweelinck and Scheidt in the North, and Frescobaldi in the South. Both Sweelinck and Frescobaldi were virtuoso players; and the organs available to them suggest an affinity with the music they wrote and played. Also, such instruments give the modern player an inkling of the differences between the organs of different geographical areas, even in the same general era. Such features as the minimal pedal divisions of these organs provide clues for appropriate registration in present-day performance. Keyboard compass was usually less than four octaves, often with the "short" bottom octave (against which Bach argued), and pedal ranges were frequently rudimentary, especially in French and southern European instruments.

---

[1]Date given by Renato Lunelli in his preface to the reprint edition of Constanzo Antegnati, *L'Arte organica*. The organ was restored in 1956 according to the plan of L. F. Tagliavini by Armando Maccarinelli. Although only the casework of most of his organs is said to remain, Antegnati, according to his own listing in his book, built well over a hundred organs in Italy between *c.* 1570 and 1605. He was born in 1549 and died in 1624, and was succeeded by his son, Giovan Francesco (born 1587), who was succeeded by his son, Graziado (born 1609), the last of the Antegnati organ builders. *L'Arte organica* is of great importance not only for organ builders but also for players, since it consists of "A Dialogue between Father and Son" dealing with registration appropriate to Antegnati's organs, as well as with organ building.

5. TOLEDO, CATHEDRAL ("EMPEROR'S ORGAN")

Juan Gaytan, 1549.[1]

Bottom Keyboard

Flautado 26 palmos[2]
Violon 26
Flautado de 13
Octava (4')
Trompeta Real (8')
  (en chamade)
Clarin de Campana (4')
  (en chamade)
Clarin Claro (4') (en chamade)
Clarin Brillante (2')
  (en chamade)
Trompeta magna (16')
  (en chamade) (treble only)

Top Keyboard

Flautado 26
Flautado 13
Violon de 13
Octava (4')
Octava tapada (4')
Flauta traversera (8')
  (treble only)
Docena y Quincena (2⅔', 2')

Top Keyboard (continued)

Quincena (2')
Nasardos V
Nasardos VIII
Lleno VIII
Corneta VII-XIII
Trompeta magna (16')
  (treble only)
Trompeta Real (8')
Bojoncillo y Clarin (8' and 4')
Violetas (8')

Pedal (with double keys)

(Front keys)
Contras de 52
Contras (16', metal)
Contras (16', wood)
Contras en Octava (4')
(Back keys)
Contras (2')
Contras (1')
Bombarda (16')
Clarines (2')
Clarines Reales (8')

---

[1]This organ is discussed in Andersen, *Orgelbogen,* p. 146, and in Rupp, *Die Entwicklungsgeschichte der Orgelbaukunst,* p. 447.

[2]*Palmos,* as the name suggests, measures in terms of the dimensions of the hand rather than the foot; 13, 26, 52 indicate 8', 16' and 32' pitch, although the lowest note of very old organs may be other than CC.

Flautado in this disposition indicates Principal tone, not flute tone (Andersen, *op. cit.,* p. 446).

Although the Spanish music of Antonio de Cabezón (1510-1566) is now played less frequently than other styles, even a brief look at this disposition from the Cathedral in Toledo (which also contains two other organs) helps the player to realize the gulf which separates the Spanish organs from those of other countries. Two later organs, one in Segovia Cathedral (1718, but altered much later), and one in the Royal Palace, Madrid (Bosch, 1778), were examined and played by the writer in 1958. These instruments display the same general kind of disposition, relying on masses of sound from brilliant, fast-speaking reed pipes, many mounted *en chamade;* in the Segovia instrument, some of these reeds speak directly at the player (into the choir), while others speak into the ambulatory, thus making possible antiphonal registration of a sort peculiar to the Spanish repertoire. Pedals are often very rudimentary: the Royal Palace organ has a 16-note pedal board, with only one 16' stop (a flute). Obviously, coupling was intended, but, as in the French instruments, pedal parts were less complicated than in northern European music. Almost invariably, all stops draw for treble and bass separately.

The famous "Emperor's Organ" described above still exists, although it is not at present playable (according to E. Power Biggs, who visited the Cathedral in Toledo in 1956); a second organ built in the 19th century is used instead. Available information suggests that the Gaytan instrument has not suffered extensive changes.

6. MEXICO CITY, CATHEDRAL

Anonymous builder, *c.* 1688-1696.[1]

Great *(treble)* c♯—d‴

Flautado de 26	16' Open, wood
Flautado Major	8' Narrow fronts
Flautado Nave	8' Wide fronts
Flauta Traversera	8' Open wood flute
Violon	8' Bourdon
Corneta Magna	8' Grand Cornet 8-12-15-15-17-17
Corneta en Ecos	8' Echo Cornet 8-12-15-15-17-17(in box)
Octava Clara	4' Narrow
Octava Nasarda	4' Wide
Espigueta	4' Rohrflute
Docena Clara	2⅔' Narrow
Docena Nasarda	2⅔' Wide, 2 ranks
Quincena Clara	2' Narrow
Quincena Nasarda	2' Wide
Diez y Setena Nasarda	1⅓' Narrow
Diez y Novena Clara	1⅗' Wide, 2 ranks
Lleno	V Plein Jeu 8-12-15-17-19
Sobre Simbala	III Mixture 15-17-22
Simbala	II Cymbal 15-19 (very narrow)
Trompa Magna	8'(?) Trumpet
Rochela	III Reed mixture (chamade)
Oboe	II Reed mixture (chamade)
Clarin Claro	III Reed mixture (chamade)

Great *(bass)* CC, DD—c'

Flautado de 26	16' Open, wood	Octava Clara	4' Narrow
Flautado Major	8' Narrow fronts	Octava Nasarda	4' Wide
Flautado Nave	8' Wide fronts	Espigueta	4' Rohrflute
Violon	8' Bourdon	Docena Clara	2⅔' Narrow

[1]The information published here was furnished by Charles Fisk, who also supplied the suggested English nomenclature and description of the pipes.

52

Great (bass) (continued)

Docena Nasarda	2⅔' Wide
Quincena Clara	2' Narrow
Quincena Nasarda	2' Wide
Espigueta	2' Rohrflute
Diez y Setena Nasarda	1⅗' Wide
Diez y Novena	1⅓' Narrow
Viente y Docena Clara	1' Narrow
Viente y Docena Nasarda	1' Wide

Lleno	V Plein Jeu 22-26-29-31-33
Sobre Simbala	III Mixture 26-29-33
Simbala	II Cymbel 33-37
Trompa Magna	8'(?) Trumpet
Bajoncillo	8' Fagotto (half length)
Chirimia	8' Krummhorn " "
Bajoncillo	8' Fagotto " "
Clarin en Quincena	2' Clarion
Orlo	III Reed Mixture 8-4-2

Brustwerk (treble)

Corneta en Eco
Flautado Major
Violon
Lleno
Tolosana
Docena Clara
Octava Clara

Ruckpositive (treble)

Corneta Magna
Fabiolete
Quincena Clara
Diez y Setena Clara

Brustwerk (bass)

Diez y Setena Clara
Diez y Novena Clara
Lleno
Octava Clara
Violon
Docena Clara

Ruckpositive (bass)

Octava Clara
Quincena Clara
Diez y Setena Clara

Pararitos
Tambores
Campanos
Cascabeles

Mr. Fisk comments on this instrument:

"The request to Spain for the Spanish organ is dated 1688; we have been unable to determine exactly when this instrument was completed, although the inscription '1696' appears on the archway just below it. Both organs were dedicated in 1736 (the second being a companion instrument in the Cathedral, apparently copied from the Spanish one).

"We chose to limit our detailed observations to the Spanish organ. We found it consists of three independent divisions: a Great, a Choir and a Pedal. These are controlled by two manuals, each of 50-note compass, CC, DD—d‴, and but ten pedal notes, CCC, DDD, EEE—BBB, i.e., one short octave. The manual keys are similar to our own; even the spacing between the two manuals is not far from A.G.O. standard. The pedals, widely spaced, protrude only five inches out of the kickboard. These ten little pedals are duplicated by a short octave of ten manual pull-down keys placed just to the left of the Great (upper) manual. There are no couplers. Far to the right of the manuals is an additional 27-note keyboard which plays a small echo organ. Both manual departments of the organ are divided uniformly into half-stops, in the manner of a reed organ. All bass half-stops are controlled by drawknobs to the left of the keyboards, while the treble half-stops are drawn on the right. For all stops, the break between bass and treble occurs between middle C and C♯. About half of the stops run the full gamut, that is, have a matching bass and treble."

Unfortunately, this magnificent instrument is unrestored and unplayable at present.

7. WORCESTER, CATHEDRAL

Thomas Dallam, 1613-1614.[1]

Great (probably C-c''')

Open Diapason I (metal) 8'
Open Diapason II (metal) 8'
Principal I (metal) 4'
Principal II (metal) 4'
Twelfth (metal) 2⅔'
Fifteenth I (metal) 2'
Fifteenth II (metal) 2'
Recorder (stopt metal) 8'

Chaire (probably F-a''')

Diapason (stopt wood) 8'
Principal (metal) 4'
Fifteenth (metal) 2'
Twenty-second (metal) 1'
Flute (stopt wood) 4'

No pedal board

---

[1]This information is from Thurston Dart's description in *Musica Britannica*, Vol. V, p. xvi (London: Stainer & Bell, 1955), based on contemporary documents; although the instrument no longer survives, knowledge of its resources is useful in understanding appropriate registration for music of the English virginalists. This instrument was used by Thomas Tomkins when he was organist at the Cathedral. A possible explanation for the English term "Chaire" is that the top of the case of this division, on the gallery rail, provided a place for the organist to sit when he played on the "great" organ. The conversion into the present-day term "choir" is perhaps a misunderstanding, based on the French term *choir*.

8. CAPPEL (with Rückpositiv), 1679

Originally built for the St. Johannes Kirche, Hamburg,
and moved to Cappel in 1816.[1]

Hauptwerk

Principal 8′
Quintadena 16′
Gedeckt Rohrflöte 8′
Octav 8′
Spitzflöte 4′
Rauschpfeife 4′
Nasard 2⅔′
Gemshorn 2′
Mixtur V-VI
Cymbel III
Trompet 8′

Rückpositiv

Principal 4′
Gedeckt 8′
Quintadena 8′
Sesquialtera II
Rohrflöte 4′
Octav 2′
Tertian II
Sifflöte 1⅓′
Scharff IV-VI
Dulzian 16′

Pedal

Untersatz 16′
Octav 8′
Octav 4′
Nachthorn 2′
Rauschpfeife II
Mixtur IV-VI
Posaune 16′
Trompet 8′
Kornett 2′

---

[1]Disposition by courtesy of Mrs. Agaath van Leeuwerik. M. A. Vente says
that this organ has some pipes which predate the Schnitger instrument of
1679.

9. STEINKIRCHEN (with Brustwerk), 1687

Restored by Rudolph von Beckerath, 1955.[1]

Hauptwerk
Quintadena 16'
Principal 8'
Rohrflöte 8'
Oktave 4'
Nasat 2⅔'
Oktave 2'
Gemshorn 2'
Mixtur IV-VI 1⅓'
Cimbel III
Trompete 8'
Sesquialtera II

Brustwerk
Gedeckt 8'
Rohrflöte 4'
Quinte 2⅔'
Oktave 2'
Spitzflöte 2'
Tertian II
Scharf III-V ⅔'
Krummhorn 8'
Tremulant

Pedal
Principal 16'
Oktave 8'
Oktave 4'
Nachthorn 2'
Mixtur IV-V 1⅓'
Rauschpfeife 2⅔'
Posaune 16'
Trompete 8'
Kornett 2'

Manual Coupler

Cimbelstern

---

[1]Disposition and photograph (Plate IV) by courtesy of Rudolph von Beckerath, who also provided the following information: In 1720 the present Sesquialtera replaced an original Rauschpfeife; the Quinte 2⅔' is believed by the restorer to have been originally a Quinte 1⅓'. The present Pedal Mixtur is by Mr. von Beckerath, since the original one had been replaced in 1720 by a Quinte 6' (5⅓').

57

10. NOORDBROEK (with Rugwerk), HERVORMDE KERK, 1698

Hoofdwerk	Rugwerk	Pedaal
Quintadena 16′	Gedeckt 8′	Bourdon 16′
Praestant 8′	Praestant 4′	Praestant 8′
Holpijp 8′	Fluit 4′	Gedeckt 8′
Octaaf 4′	Octaaf 2′	Octaaf 4′
Spitsfluit 4′	Scherp III-IV	Bazuin 16′
Quint 2⅔′	Sesquialtera II-III	Trompet 8′
Octaaf 2′	Dulciaan 8′	Klaroen 4′
Mixtuur IV-V 1′		
Trompet 8′	COUPLERS: Rugwerk to Hoofdwerk	
Vox Humana 8′	Hoofdwerk to Pedaal	

These three instruments, all of which are in a reasonably good state of repair and at least two of which (Steinkirchen and Noordbroek) have been conscientiously restored, form a highly instructive trio for illustrating both the uniformity and the variety of the Schnitger scheme. This is especially evident in the careful relation of the disposition of each division to its basic stop: for instance, on the Noordbroek organ,[1] which has no 16′ Principal in the Pedal, the 8′ Principal is referred to as "Praestant," whereas in the Steinkirchen organ the 8′ is called "Oktave," due to the presence of a 16′ as the basic stop. (The Dutch term for the basic stop is usually "Praestant," the German term, "Principal." Plates III, IV and VI will help in comparing case heights and in noting the presence of a Brustwerk at Steinkirchen in comparison to the Rückpositiv at Cappel and Noordbroek.

Noordbroek lacks a second mixture in the main division, while the two larger instruments have Cimbels added after the regular Mixtur, probably to give this division complete self-sufficiency without the need to couple. Also, the smaller instrument omits the mixture in the Pedal, but retains the reeds, while the other two have both mixture and reeds. Typical of the Schnitger work in every case known to the writer is the complete chorus on each division insofar as the size of the total organ permits, based on 8′, 4′, or 2′ in the manuals, and on 8′ or 16′ in the pedal divisions.

---

[1]Boumann, *Orgels in Nederland*, p. 74. When visited by the writer in 1956, this organ was being restored by local workers using some new pipes, including the 2′ Octaaf, Sesquialtera, and Scherp made by Stinkens, and a 16′ Quintadena made by Flentrop. The reeds, assertive and clear, are said to be the original ones.

11. ZWOLLE, MICHAELSKERK

Arp and Frans Caspar Schnitger, 1718-1721; restored, 1953-1955, by D. A. Flentrop, Zaandam.

This is the instrument taken as a model in the next discussion, both because its size and disposition make it the most extensive example extant of the work of the Schnitger family, and because it is such an exceptional example of a conscientious restoration carried out with infinite regard for detail.

Hoofdwerk	*Bovenpositief*
Prestant 16′	Prestant 8′
Quintadena 16′	Holpijp 8′
Octaaf 8′	Viola 8′ *
Roerfluit 8′	Quinta 6′ (5⅓′)
Speelfluit 4′	Octaaf 4′
Nasaat 3′ (2⅔′)	Holfluit 4′
Superoctaaf 2′	Quinta 3′ (2⅔′)
Cimbel III	Superoctaaf 2′
Ruispijp II (2′, 1⅓′)	Woudfluit 2′
Mixtuur VI	Sifflet 1½′ (1⅓′)
Trompet 16′	Tertiaan II
Trompet 8′	Scherp V
Vox Humana 8′	**Viool di Gamba 8′ (reed)**
	Trompet 4′

---

*The only 19th-century stop left in the organ after its restoration.

Rugwerk	Borstwerk	Pedaal
Prestant 8′	Fluitgedeckt 8′	Prestant 16′
Quintadena 8′	Prestant 4′	Subbas 16′
Roerfluit 8′	Roerfluit 4′	Octaaf 8′
Octaaf 4′	Spitsfluit 3′ (2⅔′)	Holpijp 8′
Fluit 4′	Superoctaaf 2′	Superoctaaf 4′
Quintfluit 3′ (2⅔′)	Gemshoorn 2′	Vlakfluit 2′
Superoctaaf 2′	Quintanus 1½′(1⅓′)	Mixtuur VIII
Sesquialtera II	Nachthoorn 1′	Fagot 32′
Scherp IV	Sesquialtera II	Bazuin 16′
Cimbel III	Mixtuur IV	Trompet 8′
Fagot 16′	Dulciaan 8′	Trompet 4′
Schalmei 8′	Regaal 8′	Cornet 2′
Tremulant (also af- fecting Hoofdwerk)	Tremulant	

All manuals can be coupled to Hoofdwerk, which can be coupled to the Pedaal. Wind pressure, 3.38″, slightly higher (3.9″) on the Pedaal.

Mixture composition[1] (pitches at CC of lowest rank):
        Hoofdwerk: Ruispijp, 2′; Mixtuur, 1⅓′; Cimbel, ⅕′
        Rugwerk: Cimbel, ⅙′; Scherp, ½′
        Borstwerk: Mixtuur, ½′
        Bovenpositief: Tertiaan, ⅘′ and ⅔′; Scherp, ⅔′
        Pedaal: Mixtuur, 2′

The Zwolle organ and the organ in the Jacobikirche in Hamburg constitute the largest extant examples of Schnitger work. The Jacobikirche organ predates Zwolle by thirty-one years (built 1688-1692), and was almost completely the work of Arp Schnitger himself (whereas Zwolle owes its original design to him, its enlargement and execution to his son); however, the Zwolle organ is in a better state of restoration, and has not suffered the ravages of war. The Hamburg organ has been moved from its initial place to another position in the church, and some unsympathetic changes have been made.

---

[1]For further details, see D. A. Flentrop, "The Schnitger Organ in the Grote Kerk at Zwolle," *Organ Institute Quarterly,* Summer, 1957.

The Zwolle instrument, in the opinion of the writer, constitutes the best example available in Europe of the Schnitger ideas carried to the logical conclusion in an instrument of monumental proportions. Moreover, the conscientious restoration recently carried out, the exceptional reconstruction of the action, and the remarkable acoustics of the church make this instrument an extraordinarily satisfactory one for the player.

Again, the Schnitger practice of basing each division on a given Principal pitch is clearly evident, and each division is in its own case with an extensive complement of reeds, flutes, and stops of individual character. The Hoofdwerk is based on 16′, carrying a 2′—1⅓′ Ruispijp as the beginning of the off-unison stops for the ensemble (in addition to a 2⅔′ stop of rather wide scale, which indicates that it was intended primarily for use in solo line playing), the 1⅓′ Mixtuur and Cimbel (⅕′) completing the gamut of pitches, when the 8′, 4′, and 2′ voices are added.

The Bovenpositief is based on an 8′ pitch, carrying a 2⅔′ voice with a Scherp (Scharff) which has different breaks and a slightly lower pitch in some registers than the Scherp of the Rugwerk.

The Borstwerk, based on 4′ pitch, has the highest Mixture of all, while the Rugwerk, based on 8′ (with a 16′ half-length reed also intended for the full chorus), has a higher Scherp than the Bovenpositief, and a higher secondary Mixture (Cimbel, ⅙′).

The doubling of 2′ pitches on several divisions, one a flute scale, the other a Principal scale, is to provide variety in intensity in different combinations, and it is unlikely that both of these (or two flue stops of any given pitch) were intended to be employed simultaneously in the full chorus.

The Pedaal reverts to a 2′ Mixture, comparable to that of the Hoofdwerk. The only apparent reason for the omission of a Principal of 32′ pitch was the low ceiling height above the case. The bottom octave of the 32′ Bazuin is half-length, a condition which usually required the name of "Fagot" for such a stop with Schnitger; this stop was added by Frans Caspar Schnitger, and was not in the original disposition. A significant curiosity about the Pedaal disposition is the omission of a 2′ or a 2⅔′ Ruispijp to fill the niche between the Mixtuur and the rest of the chorus. However, playing the organ suggests that this is omitted because of the unusually resonant acoustics of the church, since the Pedaal chorus has a sound which is completely satisfactory in fullness, intensity, and clarity.

61

Disposition der Stimmen einer Neuen Orgel, so sich sehr füeglich in der Schönen St. Michaelis Kirchen alhier in der Stadt Zwoll, Nach der selben Gühte proportion sich schicken könten,

Stimmen	In Ober-Manual	pijpen
1	Præstant — — — — 16 Voet	49
	Van Engels Tin groß Güntgen, sichte, C G D E F Fis sprecken mit in der Quintadena,	
2	Quintadena — — — 16 Voet	49
3	Octav — — — — 8 Voet	49
4	Rohrflöit — — — 8 Voet	49
5	Octav — — — — 4 Voet	49
6	Spielflöit — — — 4 Voet	49
7	Nasat — — — — 3 Voet	49
8	Rauschpfeiffe — — 2 Starck	98
9	Mixtur 4·5·6· Starck	245
10	Cimbel — — — 3 Starck	147
11	Trommet — — — 16 Voet	49
12	Trommet — — — 8 Voet	49
13	Vox humana — — 8 Voet	49

Stimmen	In ünter-Manual	pijpen
14	Præstant — — — 8 Voet	49
	Van Engels Tin, groß Dintgen, sichte, C E sprecken mit int	
15	Gedact — — — 8 Voet	49
16	Vil de Gamba — 8 Voet	49
17	Octav — — — 4 Voet	49
18	Quinta — — — 3 Voet	49
19	Waldflöit — — 2 Voet	49
20	Super Octav — 2 Voet	49
21	Hollflöit — — 4 Voet	49
22	Tertian — — 2 Starck	98
23	Sieflöit — — 1½ Voet	49
24	Scharf 4·5·6· Starck	245
25	Dulcian — — 8 Voet	49

Stimmen	Im Rückpositiv	pijpen
26	Præstant — — 8 Voet	49
	Van Engels Tin Geheel int Gesichte	
27	Quintadena — 8 Voet	49
28	Flöite dües — 8 Voet	49

1960

Stimmen	Transport voriges	pijpen
	daren sint — — —	1960
29	Principal — 4 Voet	49
30	Flöite dües — 2 Voet	49
31	Quint flöit — 3 Voet	49
32	Octav — — 2 Voet	49
33	Sexquialt — 2 Starck	98
34	Scharp — 4 Starck	196
35	Hoboÿ — 8 Voet	49

	Im Pedal	
36	Præstant — 16 Voet	27
	Van Engels Tin Geheel int Gesichte	
37	Octav — 8 Voet	27
38	Rohr Quinta — 12 Voet	27
39	Octav — 4 Voet	27
40	Rauschpfeiffe — 2 Starck	54
41	Mixtur — 6 Starck	162
42	Nachthorn — 2 Voet	27
43	Posaunen — 16 Voet	27
44	Trommet — 8 Voet	27
45	Schalmeÿ — 4 Voet	27
46	Cornet — 2 Voet	27

Hier Ventiel tot 2 Tremulanten:

Hier 120 5 schleif windladen 2958 daer vorgemelte Stimmen up tho staan kamen, mit 8 Blaß Balgen, à 8 Voet lang 4 Voet breet, mit ihre windleijdungen ferner drij Clavier van Elvene bein und Eben Holtz die semitonia von C G D E F Fis etc: biß F in allen 49 Claves Ein Pedal Clavier von C G D E F etc: biß D tho Sahmen 27 Claves alle angehenge und sehdern van Messing und Kopperdrath, alle Præstanten van Klaren Engels Tin Well gebrunert. tho alle dat jn wendige pijpwerck sal up 1000 tt loth 400 tt Tin versettet wurden;

Wantla

The original disposition for the organ in the Michaelskerk, Zwolle,

Wann tho diesen Orgelbuw de Orgelmacher tho syn arbeit soll alle Mathe-
rialen: als dass Wagenschott tho die 5 Windladen, 8 Blassbälgen, Cangle
und windröhren, Registratur abstractur, mit den Ganzen ingebau der
Orgel, sthem tin, loth, Messing, Kopper, messing und Kopperdrath, mit ben
techleder, daer de windladen mit gefordert, und die bälgen mit betrocken
werden, Iser werk tho gantze Regierung, und Schruben dar de windladen
mit tho sahmen schrasen worden, snurung tho Giesen, und Kohlen tho
löhten, Kersen, Pargament tho de windladen und bälgen, liem, Messing,
belis etc. Tuchtich und güth verschaffen, und solche arbeit
allen stucken durabel und Eerlich verfertiget, so dass bey über liefe-
rung die selbe, so woll von de Herren liebhabers von der Musique, als
auch von verständige Organisten sol vor güth erkant und gepriesen
worden, wil vor Gemeltes Orgelwerk, nach Grauer überlegung Kamen
tho Kosten de Summa van 1495 Caroli Gülders.

De Stadt Zwoll let dass fundament daer de Orgel up sthahn soll, mit
die strockur, Balg Haus, und Bildhauer arbeit verfertigen, und
besorgen den Orgelmacher ein Plats da er sein arbeit verrichten
Kan Halten darby den Bolgen Treter, und haben als dan darmit
Nichtes tho schaffen.

Solches Habe Einen Hoch Edlen Hoch Achtbahren Magistrat
der Stadt Zwoll, nobenst Presentirung Meine gehorsahme dienste,
schüldig stermassen überreichen sollen, der ich verbleibe

Dero Salv: Titt: Titt:

Zwoll den 23 decemb:
1718.

unter thänigster
diener.

Arp Schnitger.
Orgelmacher

dated 1718, signed by Arp Schnitger.

The Pedaal reeds have the great power and clarity typical of Schnitger, although they had to be largely reconstructed. Their authenticity of sound is another remarkable feature in this organ when it is compared to other Schnitger instruments with reeds said to be unrestored. How authentic or original a reed stop can be is a matter of some conjecture, due to the wear and tear on the reed tongue, the mishandling in tuning, etc.; but the reed registers which are thought to be original coincide in quality and intensity with the restored ones, and this is the main assurance to the builder or player that they are as near as we are likely to come to the right sound. Another assurance is the fact that these reeds fit logically into the full sound from the flue chorus.

The profusion of solo reed voices is noteworthy, and there is great variety in quality and intensity. Also, the inclusion of a Sesquialtera or a Tertiaan (an octave higher) on three of four manual divisions is typical of the preference of Schnitger and his contemporaries for this solo voice. (Usually the register goes no lower than A or c'.)

Finally, the presence of two tremulants on the organ, one affecting the Borstwerk and another affecting the Rugwerk, Hoofdwerk, and Pedaal, indicates that these devices were known and used in important instruments.

The restoration of the organ at Zwolle represents an exceptionally careful attempt to follow the wishes of the original builder. D. A. Flentrop, brought up as a player as well as an organ builder, is probably Europe's most experienced craftsman in the field of 18th-century restoration, and is a specialist in the work of the Schnitger family. Stops which were missing at Zwolle (due to 19th-century alterations) were copied from similar ones in the sister instrument at Alkmaar (1725), and extensive experiments were conducted to determine the scales and the voicing techniques originally employed. All but one of the registers added in the 19th century were discarded.

The original wind supply system was retained and the old pressures were restored, with the addition of only one regulator (for the Rugwerk). The Zwolle town archives produced much important documentation, including the original contract, with Arp Schnitger's signature and Vincent Lübeck's testimonial; the utmost care was taken by Flentrop to identify what remained of the original instrument, and what had to be renewed or replaced. A special feature of the Zwolle organ is its light action, utilizing Schnitger's leverage principles. Before the restoration, neglect and unsympathetic changes had rendered the action impossibly stiff.

12. MARMOUTIER

Built 1710; enlarged, 1726, by Johann Andreas Silbermann[1];
restored, 1955, by Mühleisen, Strasbourg.[2]

Hauptwerk	*Rückpositiv*	*Echo* (*from middle* C)
Bourdon 16'	Bourdon 8'	Bourdon 8'
Prinzipal 8'	Prinzipal 4'	Oktav 4'
Octav 4'	Octav 2'	Quinte 2⅔'
Octav 2'	Quinte 2⅔'	Octav 2'
Quinte 2⅔'	Mixtur III	Terz 1⅗'
Terz 1⅗'	Terz 1⅗'	
Cornet V	Cromorne 8'	*Pedal*
Mixtur III		
Zimbel III		Flotbass 16'
Trompet 8'		Oktavbass 8'
Clairon 4'	COUPLER: Rückpositiv	Flûte 4'
Vox Humana 8'	Hauptwerk (no manual to Pedal coupler)	Posaune 16'
		Trompet 8'

This beautiful instrument was well restored when played by the writer
in 1956; like the Müller instruments (Beverwijk, Haarlem, Oude Kerk in
Amsterdam), it shows a turning away from the consistent fundamentals of
the Schnitger tradition. Most conspicuous at Marmoutier is the greatly
reduced scope of the Pedal disposition. The "Echo," inspired by French
ideas of the time, was obviously intended mainly as a solo division and
not for ensemble playing. In spite of the beautiful sound of the instrument and its fine acoustical environment, registration problems arise
when it is being played, especially in the longer works of Bach, because
of the lack of a third chorus and especially because of the limited Pedal.
Conversely, the French compositions of the time (Daquin, etc.) present
a minimum of problems—and they are almost certainly the repertoire
for which the builder intended the organ.

---

[1]His work preceded that of his brother, Gottfried, the friend of Bach.
Nearly all of Gottfried Silbermann's remaining work is located in East
Germany.

[2]It is likely that German instead of French terminology was used for stops
in this organ ("Posaune" in place of "Bombarde," "Terz" for "Tierce," etc.).

13. LEIPZIG, PAULINERKIRCHE

Built 1716.[1]

Haupt Werck (middle keyboard)

Gross-Principal 16' (pure tin)
Quintadena 16'
Klein Principal 8'
Octava 4'
Octavina 2'
Gemshorn 8'
Chalumeau 8'
Flûte d'Allemagne 8'
Waldflöthe 2'
Quinta auf Principal 3'
Nassat 3'
Cornetti III
Zinck II
Gross-Mixtur V-VI

Seiten Werck (bottom keyboard)

Principal 4'
Lieblich Gedackt (Holtz) 8'
Quintadena 8'
Flûte douce 8'
Quintadecima 4'
Hohlflöthe 2'
Decima nona 3'
Vigesima nona 1½'
Weite Pfeiffe 1'
Viola 2'
Sertin 8'
Hellee Cymbel II
Mixtur IV

Pedal

Principal Bass 16' (pure tin, in case) *
Gross Quintaden Bass 16' *
Jubal Bass 8'
Nachthorn Bass 8'
Grosse Hall-Quinta 6' (in case)
Octav Bass 2'
Sub-Bass 16'

Posaunen Bass 16'
Trompeta 8'
Octava 8'
Octava 4'
Quinta-Bass 3'
Hohl-Flöth Bass 1'
Mixtur VI

---

[1]From Werner David, *Bachs Orgeln,* p. 94. His source for the disposition is the "Dresdener Handschrift Nr. 76," 1736 (ed. P. Smets, Kassel, 1934). David also gives useful descriptions of several stops in this instrument as to construction and pipe materials. Note the conglomeration of French, Italian, and German terminology.
*Used in both manual and pedal.

Brust (top keyboard)

Principal 8′ (pure tin, in case)
Grossgedackt (Holtz Weit Mensur) 8′
Octava 4′
Octava 2′
Nassat 3′
Largo 1½′
Sedecima 1′
Viol di Gamba 8′
Rohr-Flöthe 4′
Schweitzer Pfeiffe 1′
Helle Cymbeln II
Mixtur III

This organ also possessed a tremulant, Cimbelstern, ventils[2] for each keyboard division and for pedal, and a pumper's warning bell.

Of this organ Werner David gives the following information: Chalumeau is a soft, covered reed stop; Flûte d'Allemagne is a narrow-scaled open wood flute, voiced very sharply; Weite Pfeiffe is a metal, wide-scaled open, sharply voiced stop; Sertin, usually called Sordun, is a covered reed stop of medium loudness; Largo is a wide-scaled metal open stop; Schweitzer Pfeiffe is a very narrow-scaled, open, sharply voiced stop; Jubal Bass is an open flute of principal scale, but smoothly voiced; Grosse Hall-Quinta is a wide-scaled, very loud stop, with rather high cut-up. (Also from the "Dresdener Handschrift," 1736.) The organ is now very much changed.

---

[2]*Ventil* refers in 18th-century northern European organs to a mechanism whereby wind was excluded from the chest until a knob was drawn by the player. Though not always provided, ventil (meaning "valve") arrangements were not unusual, especially on large organs, perhaps as a means for conserving wind when a division was not in use.

14. PARIS, ST. GERVAIS

(as is was during François Couperin's tenure as organist, 1687-1723)[1]

Grand Orgue (C-c‴)
(second keyboard)

Montre 16′
Bourdon 16′
Prestant 4′
Doublette 2′
Fourniture IV
Cymbale III
Flûte 4′
   (removed, 1714)
Grosse Tierce 3⅕′
Nasard 2⅔′
Quarte (?)
Tierce 1⅗′
Trompette 8′
Clairon 4′
Voix Humaine 8′
Cornet V (2 octaves)

Positiv (C-c‴)
(first keyboard)

Bourdon 8′
Montre 4′
Flûte 4′
Doublette 2′
Fourniture III
Cymbale III
Nasard 2⅔′
Tierce 1⅗′
Larigot 1⅓′

Récit (25 *or* 32 *notes,*
g-c‴)
(third keyboard)

Cornet Séparé V
Trompette 8′
   (added, 1714)

Echo(37 *notes,* c-c‴)
(fourth keyboard)

Bourdon 8′ et
   Flûte 4′
Cymbale III
Nasard 2⅔′
Doublette 2′ et
   Tierce 1⅗′
Cromorne 8′
   (Bass octave of this
   division removed,
   1714)

Pédale (29 *notes,*
A, C, D, E, *to* e)

Flûte 8′
Flûte 4′
Trompette 8′

COUPLERS: Grand Orgue Positiv
Grand Orgue to Pédale

Tremblant doux   Tremblant fort

---

[1]Couperin was succeeded by his sons. As was often the case, several builders worked on this organ up to and including the time of Couperin; at least ten builders have made changes in it up to the present day, the most illus-

The changes in this organ since Couperin's time and the 1714 alterations by François Thierry include case alterations (1758-1759) by Pierre-Claude Thiessé, who added decorations and relocated some pipes; between 1764 and 1768 François Henri Clicquot relocated several registers and added new stops, replacing some registers; his additions or replacements included the 16′, 8′ and 4′ reeds now to be found in the organ.[2]

It is worth noting that earlier organs by the Clicquot family, such as that in the Versailles Palace Chapel (Robert Clicquot, 1711),[3] are relevant to Couperin's music, since the present St. Gervais organ (now with five keyboards!) has been so much changed.[4] It still contains most of the pipework of Couperin's instrument, however, and when examined and played by the writer in 1959 was dazzling to both eye and ear.

---

trious being François Henri Clicquot who made extensive alterations in 1768. During Couperin's time the organ was cared for by Alexander Thierry; the 1714 alterations were made by Thierry, apparently at Couperin's request or at least with his permission. A restoration was carried out in 1921, after war damage, under the direction of Paul Brunold, apparently to return the organ to its state of 1768. See Hardouin, *Le Grand-Orgue de St.-Gervais à Paris,* pp. 3, 14 ff.

[2]Hardouin, *op. cit.*

[3]Restored about 1952 by Gonzalez, Paris, under supervision of Norbert Dufourcq.

[4]Hardouin states that, because of Couperin's explicit directions for registration in his organ works (the two Masses), the St. Gervais organ has special importance for the player.

15. BEVERWIJK, GROTE KERK, 1756

Hoofdwerk

Prestant 8'
Octaav 4'
Superoctaav 2'
Quint 2⅔'
Roerfluit 8'
Mixtuur IV-VI
Sesquialter II
Trompet 8'

Bovenwerk

Prestant 16' (from middle C)
Hohlfluit 8'
Quintadeen 8'
Gemshoorn 4'
  (new, Flentrop, 1936)
Fluit 2'
Cornet IV (from middle C)
Vox Humana 8'
Viool da Gamba 8' (originally
  Dulciaan 8'; changed in the
  19th century)

Pedaal

Bourdon 16'
Prestant 8'
Octaav 4'
Woudfluit 2'
Fagot 16'
Trompet 8'

Pedal Coupler

Manual Coupler (divided at middle C)

The Beverwijk organ is another fine instrument which illustrates, as do some Silbermann organs, the beginning of the decadence in organ design (when compared to Schnitger). For example, the Beverwijk organ has no separating walls between Pedaal and Hoofdwerk cases; the Mixtuur on the Hoofdwerk is an amazing one: it is extremely low in pitch ($5\frac{1}{3}'$ at middle C); there is no mixture on the second division, nor is there one on the Pedaal; the 16′ Prestant from middle C on the Bovenwerk is also a departure; and finally, the case is partially attached to the back gallery wall, rather than free-standing.

The instrument was restored in 1936 by H. W. Flentrop, the father of D. A. Flentrop. At that time, the reed resonators were in such bad condition that they had to be renewed. This was done by taking the scales, melting down the metal, and replacing the old resonators with new ones made of the original metal and to the original scales. The reed boots were retained.[1]

Registration problems in the Bach repertoire become rather formidable on the Beverwijk organ, as they do on the Silbermann instrument at Marmoutier. However, the writer found this a magnificent instrument to play, partly because it includes perhaps the most beautiful Sesquialter in Europe and a remarkable Cornet. Again, the reduced Pedaal disposition causes problems in pieces requiring a supporting contrapuntal line, and it is necessary to resort to coupling.

---

[1]Restoration information by courtesy of D. A. Flentrop.

16. A CABINET ORGAN by JOHN SNETZLER

London, *c.* 1748; now the property of Colonial Williamsburg, Virginia.

One keyboard, divided at middle C

Fifteenth
Twelfth
Principal 4′
Open Diapason (treble only)
Flute 4′ (not divided)
Stopt Diapason 8′ (not divided)

This organ, restored in 1953 by the London builder Noel Mander, was in Kimberley Hall, Norwich, until it was acquired by Mr. Mander. It boasts an elegant "sandwich" keyboard of ebony and ivory, and has all of its original pipes. Although it lacks the signature of its builder, Mr. Mander, who has made a special study of Snetzler's work, authenticates it completely. This instrument exemplifies the resources which were available to Handel for his concerto performances.

17. A CABINET ORGAN by J. STRÜMPHLER

Amsterdam, 1781; now the property of the Netherlands Bach Society and located in the Vituskerk, Naarden.[1]

One keyboard, divided at middle C

Holpijp 8′ (not divided)
Viola 8′ (treble only)
Prestant 4′
Fluit 4′
Quint 3′ (2⅔′)
Nachthoorn 2′
Octaaf 2′
Sexa (Sesquialtera, treble only)

This instrument is perhaps the finest cabinet organ in existence. The keyboard, as was typical of the time, slides inside the case, giving the instrument the appearance of a closed desk. It has the original keyboard and all of its original pipes. In 1951 it was restored by D. A. Flentrop.

These instruments, fashionable in the second half of the 18th century, are not to be confused with the earlier one-manual instruments, like the one at Oosthuizen (1521), which were *koororgels* — much louder sounding and intended for use in churches. Cabinet organs were especially popular in England, where many were made by Snetzler; there are several in the workshop of Noel Mander in London, including one reportedly owned by King George III and played by Handel.[2]

The Handel concerto repertoire is admirably suited to these instruments, while the works of Sweelinck and Scheidt are more at home on the earlier instruments at Oosthuizen and Alkmaar (Laurenskerk koororgel).

---

[1]A comparison of the photograph (Plate X) with the disposition will clarify the case size and its relation to the open 4′ stop.

[2]In the United States, there are Snetzler cabinet organs in the Yale University Museum, in Colonial Williamsburg, and in the Congregational Church, South Dennis, Massachusetts.

18. PARIS, STE. CLOTHILDE

(as played by César **Franck**, 1859-1890)[1]

Grande Orgue (bottom)

Montre 16′
Bourdon 16′
Montre 8′
Gambe 8′
Flûte Harmonique 8′
Bourdon 8′
Prestant 4′
Octave 4′
Quinte 2⅔′
Doublette 2′
Plein Jeu V
Bombarde 16′
Trompette 8′
Clairon 4′

Positiv (middle)

Bourdon 16′
Montre 8′
Gambe 8′
Flûte Harmonique 8′
Bourdon 8′
Salicional 8′
Prestant 4′
Flûte Octaviante 4′
Quinte 2⅔′
Doublette 2′
Clarinette 8′
Trompette 8′
Clairon 4′

Récit (top)

(enclosed)
Bourdon 8′
Flûte Harmonique 8′
Viole de Gambe 8′
Voix Céleste 8′
Flûte Octaviante 4′
Octavin 2′
Basson-Hautbois 8′
Voix Humaine 8′
Trompette 8′
Clairon 4′

Pédale

Quintaton 32′
Contrebasse 16′
Flûte 8′
Octave 4′
Bombarde 16′
Basson 16′
Trompette 8′
Clairon 4′

---

[1]Wallace Goodrich, *The Organ in France* (Boston, 1917), p. 127.

Aristide Cavaillé-Coll (1811-1899), perhaps because of his association with César Franck, nearly succeeded in establishing a new classic dimension for the organ, relying heavily on reed stops on higher wind pressures to give individuality to each division. Other features which he did not invent but employed to advantage, include various flute voices of the same pitch (especially the Bourdon and the Flûte Harmonique, an overlength, open, pierced pipe), the use of the Celeste, swell boxes, and mixtures of lower pitches. By this time, many of the elements which Schnitger considered essential were forgotten: the integrity of each division housed within a case; mixture pitches related to the basic pitch and disposition of each division; complete choruses on each division, with reeds related in pitch and scale to the ensemble. Even the slider chest and mechanical key action were losing their validity, being assisted by Barker levers using pneumatics.[2] Visually, the organ no longer displayed its basic resources in the front and in the proportions of the cases. The repertoire, especially with Franck, became less idiomatic or, at best, placed a new interpretation on the whole nature of the medium and on performance.

---

[2]C. S. Barker patented his pneumatic lever in France in 1839, where it was extensively used by Cavaillé-Coll. Henry Willis (1821-1901) developed a reliable tubular pneumatic action by 1872 (St. Paul's Cathedral, London) and utilized this action in many instruments in England.

19. BUSCH-REISINGER MUSEUM, HARVARD UNIVERSITY

The organ in the balcony of the Romanesque Hall was built in 1958 by D. A. Flentrop of Zaandam, Holland. It is a modern instrument constructed according to the tonal and mechanical principles of the classic organs of Europe.

These principles may be briefly summarized as follows:[1]

(1) Tracker action, direct mechanical linkage between key and pipe valve.

(2) Slider chests, pipes of the same note within each division standing on a common windway.

(3) Classic specification, with classic pipe voicing throughout the instrument.

(4) Low wind pressure, of $1\frac{7}{16}''$ to $2\frac{1}{16}''$.

(5) The organ free-standing (not enclosed in chambers or swell boxes) with each division (Hoofdwerk, Rugpositief, Borstwerk and Pedaal) focused by a case.

Hoofdwerk	*Rugpositief*	*Pedaal*
Prestant 8′	Holpijp 8′	Bourdon 16′
Roerfluit 8′	Prestant 4′	Prestant 8′
Octaaf 4′	Roerfluit 4′	Gedekt 8′
Speelfluit 4′	Gemshoorn 2′	Fluit 4′
Nasard 2⅔′	Quint 1⅓′	Mixtuur III Rks
Vlakfluit 2′	Mixtuur II Rks	Fagot 16′
Terts 1⅗′	Kromhoorn 8′	Trompet 8′
Mixtuur IV Rks		

Borstwerk	COUPLERS
Zingend Gedekt 8′	Hoofdwerk — Pedaal
Koppelfluit 4′	Rugpositief — Pedaal
Prestant 2′	Borstwerk — Pedaal
Sifflet 1′	Rugpositief — Hoofdwerk
Regal 8′	Borstwerk — Hoofdwerk

---

[1]Comments and disposition by courtesy of E. Power Biggs.

BIBLIOGRAPHY

Adlung, Jakob: *Musica mechanica organoedi* (written largely 1723-1727), Berlin, 1768; facsimile, Kassel: Bärenreiter, 1931

Aldrich, Putnam: *Ornamentation in J. S. Bach's Organ Works.* New York: Coleman-Ross, 1950

Andersen, Paul-Gerhardt: *Orgelbogen.* Copenhagen: Munksgaard, 1955

Antegnati, Constanzo: *L'Arte organica,* Brescia, 1608; reprint, Mainz: Rheingold-Verlag, 1941

Bach, C. P. E.: *Versuch über die wahre Art, das Clavier zu spielen,* Berlin, 1753-1762. Translated and edited by William J. Mitchell. New York: W. W. Norton, 1949

Banchieri, Adriano: *Conclusoni nel suono dell'organo,* Bologna, 1608; facsimile, Milan: *Bollettino Bibliografico Musicale,* 1934

Bedbrook, G. S.: *Keyboard Music from the Middle Ages to the Beginnings of the Baroque.* London: Macmillan, 1949

Bedos de Celles, Dom François: *L'Art du facteur d'orgues,* Paris, 1766; facsimile, Kassel: Bärenreiter, 1934

Blanton, Joseph: *The Organ in Church Design.* Albany, Texas: Venture Press, 1956

Bodky, Erwin: *The Interpretation of Bach's Keyboard Music.* Cambridge: Harvard University Press, 1960

Bornefeld, Helmut: *Orgelbau und neue Orgelmusik.* Kassel: Bärenreiter, 1952

Boumann, M. A.: *Orgels in Nederland.* Amsterdam: De Lange, 1949

Cavaillé-Coll, Aristide: "De l'Orgue et de son architecture," *Revue Générale de l'Architecture des Travaux Publics,* Paris, 1856

Cavaillé-Coll, C. et E.: *Aristide Cavaillé-Coll, ses origines, sa vie, ses oeuvres.* Paris: Fischbacher, 1929

David, Hans T., and Arthur Mendel: *The Bach Reader.* New York: W. W. Norton, 1945

77

David, Werner: *Johann Sebastian Bachs Orgeln*. Berlin: Berliner Musikinstrumenten Sammlung, 1951

Dufourcq, Norbert: *Jean Sebastien Bach*. Paris: La Colombe, 1947

Ellinwood, Leonard: *The History of American Church Music*. New York: Morehouse-Gorham, 1953

Flade, Ernest: "The Organ Builder, Gottfried Silbermann," *Organ Institute Quarterly* (Andover, Mass.), Vol. III (1953), Nos. 3 & 4; Vol. IV (1954), Nos. 1, 2, 3 & 4

Flentrop, D. A.: "Organ Building in Europe," *The Diapason* (Chicago), November & December, 1956

—: "The Schnitger Organ in the Grote Kerk at Zwolle," (translated from the Dutch by John Fesperman), *Organ Institute Quarterly*, Summer 1957

Frotscher, G.: *Geschichte des Orgelspiels*. Kassel: Bärenreiter, 1935

Goldschmidt, Erich: "Problems of Contemporary Organ Building," *Organ Institute Quarterly*, Vol. VIII (1955), Nos. 1 & 2

Gough, Hugh: "The Classical Grand Pianoforte, 1770-1830," *Proceedings of the Royal Musical Association* (London), 77th Session, 1951

Graaf, G. A. C. de: *Literatuur over het orgel*. Amsterdam: Published by the Author, 1957

Grabner, Hermann: *Die Kunst des Orgelbaues*. Berlin: Max Hesses Verlag, 1958.

Haake, Walter: *Orgeln*. Königstein im Taunus: Langwiesche,1954

Hardmeyer, Willy: *Einführung in die Schweizerische Orgelbaukunst*. Zürich: Hug, 1947

Hardouin, Pierre: *Le Grand-orgue de Saint-Gervais à Paris* (revised edition). Paris: Imprimerie du Compagnonnage, 1949

Harich-Schneider, Eta: *The Harpsichord*. St. Louis: Concordia Publishing House, 1954

Hess, Joachim: *Beschrijving van het nieuw en uitmuntend orgel in de St. Janskerk te Gouda*, Gouda, 1774; reprint, Utrecht: Wagenaar, 1945

—: *Dispositien der merkwaardigste kerkorgeln*, Gouda, 1774; facsimile, Utrecht: Wagenaar, 1945

—: *Luister van het Orgel*, Gouda, 1772; reprint, Utrecht: Wagenaar, 1945

Hickman, Hans: *Das Portativ*. Kassel: Bärenreiter, 1936

Jamison, James Blaine: *Organ Design and Appraisal*. New York: H. W. Gray, 1959

Klotz, Hans: *Das Buch von der Orgel*. Kassel: Bärenreiter, 1955
—: *Ueber die Orgelkunst*. Kassel: Bärenreiter, 1934
Lightvoet, A. W.: *Exotic and Ancient European Musical Instruments*. The Hague: Nijgh en van Ditmar, no date
Leonhardt, Gustav M.: *The Art of Fugue, Bach's Last Harpsichord Work*. The Hague: Nijhoff, 1952
Lunelli, Renato: *Der Orgelbau in Italien*. Mainz: Rheingold-Verlag, 1956
Mahrenholz, Christhard: *Die Berechnung der Orgelpfeifenmensuren von Mittelalter bis zur Mitte des neunzehnten Jahrhunderts*. Kassel: Bärenreiter, 1938
—: *Die Orgelregister*. Kassel: Bärenreiter, 1930
Münger, Fritz: *Schweizer Orgeln von der Gotik bis zur Gegenwart*. Bern: Verlag Krompholz, 1961
Orgel Monographien Serie. Mainz: Rheingold-Verlag, 1940—
Owen, Barbara: "The History of the Organ in America," brochure included with Columbia Masterworks ML 5496 (Columbia Records, New York), 1960
Phillips, Gordon: "Purcell's organs and organ music," *Organ and Choral Aspects and Prospects* (Hinrichsen's Musical Year Book, Vol. X). London and New York: Hinrichsen Edition, 1958
Praetorius, M.: *De Organographia (Syntagma Musicum, Part II)*, Wolfenbüttel, 1619; facsimile, Kassel: Bärenreiter, 1929
Quantz, Johann Joachim: *Versuch einer Anweisung, die flûte traversière zu spielen*, Berlin, 1752; facsimile, third edition of 1789, Kassel: Bärenreiter, 1953
Quoika, R.: *Altösterreichische Hornwerke*, edited by W. Supper. Berlin: Gesellschaft der Orgelfreunde, 1959
—: *Das Positiv in Geschichte und Gegenwart*. Kassel: Bärenreiter, 1957
Rihse and Seggermann: *Klingende Schätze* (Orgel-Land zwischen Elbe und Weser). Cuxhaven: Verlag Oliva, 1957
Rupp, Emile: *Die Entwicklungsgeschichte der Orgelbaukunst*. Strasbourg: Benziger, 1929
Sachs, Curt: *The History of Musical Instruments*. New York: W. W. Norton, 1940
Schlick, Arnold: *Spiegel der Orgelmacher und Organisten*, Mainz, 1511; facsimile, Kassel: Bärenreiter, 1951
Schweitzer, Albert: *Deutsche und Französische Orgelbaukunst und Orgelkunst*. Leipzig: Breitkopf und Härtel, 1927

—: *J. S. Bach,* London, 1911 (English edition); reprint, New York: Macmillan, 1949

Shewring, Walter: "Organs in Italy: Brescia and Verona," *The Organ* (London), Vol. XXXV (April, 1956), No. 140

Sigtenhorst Meyer, Bernhard van den: *Jan P. Sweelinck en zijn instrumentale muziek* (2 vols.). The Hague: Servire, 1946-1948

Stevenson, Robert: "Cathedral Organs in Capitals of Argentina, Brazil and Chile," *The Organ* (London), Vol. XLI (July 1961), No. 161

Sumner, William Leslie: "Arp Schnitger," *Organ Institute Quarterly,* Vol. V (1955), Nos. 2, 3 & 4

—: "Arp Schnitger and His Organs," *The Organ* (London), Vol. XVII (January and April, 1938)

—: *The Organ.* New York: Philosophical Library, 1953

Tagliavini, Luigi Ferdinando: "Il problema della salvaguardia e del restauro degli organi antichi," *Musica Sacra* (Milan), Anno II (September & October, 1956), No. 5

Terry, Charles Sanford: *Bach's Orchestra.* London: Oxford University Press, 1932; reprint, 1958

—: *J. S. Bach.* London: Oxford University Press, 1929

Timmerman, Henri: "Roem van een barokorgel," in *Overijssel, Jaarboek voor cultuur en historie, 1959.* Zwolle: Uitgeverij De Erven J. J. Tijl

Töpfer, Johann Gottlob: *Lehrbuch der Orgelbaukunst,* Weimar, 1855-1858; reprint, Mainz: Rheingold-Verlag, 1936-1939

The Tracker (a quarterly newsletter). York, Pa.: Organ Historical Society, 250 East Market Street. Publication began Oct., 1956

Vente, Maarten A.: *Die Brabanter Orgel in Zeitalter der Gotik und der Renaissance.* Amsterdam: H. A. Paris, 1958 [Summaries in English, Dutch and French]

Walther, Johann Gottfried: *Musikalisches Lexicon,* 1732; facsimile, Kassel: Bärenreiter, 1953

Werckmeister, Andreas: *Orgelprobe,* Frankfort, 1698; facsimile, London: Cassell, 1952

Wörsching, Joseph: *Der Orgelbauer Joseph Gabler.* Mainz: Rheingold-Verlag, 1949

—: *Der Orgelbauer Karl Riepp (1710-1775).* Mainz: Rheingold-Verlag, 1940

—: *Die Orgelbauer-Familie Silbermann in Strassburg* (in 4 parts). Mainz: Rheingold-Verlag, 1943-1949

INDEX OF ORGAN BUILDERS

81

The illustrations for the end papers are taken from *De Organographia,* Part Two of the *Syntagma Musicum* by Michael Praetorius, published in 1619. Shown are organ bellows, *Calcanten* (bellows-treaders), organ with Rückpositiv, flue pipes, and reed pipes.

The book jacket shows the nave façade of the organ in the Mexico City Cathedral. Built about 1686-1690 and imported from Spain, it is possibly the oldest organ on the North American continent.

This book was designed and printed
by The Profile Press, New York, and
bound by Stanhope Bindery, Boston